OUT
OF THE
WOODS

VOICES FROM THE FOREST CITY

AN ANTHOLOGY OF
SHORT STORIES & POEMS
BY MEMBERS OF THE
LONDON WRITERS SOCIETY

SELECTED BY
EMMA DONOGHUE

London Writers Society

Published by Indie Publishing Group Inc

DEDICATED TO

the members of the London Writers Society and,

in particular, those who rose to the challenge

and submitted their work to this project.

This is your book.

Contents

Foreword

TERRY FALLIS

I've always considered London to be a very writerly city. University towns usually are. But I find London punches above its literary weight. The annual Words Festival, which I've been lucky enough to attend on several occasions, is among the best writers' festivals I know. And the London Writers Society is a welcoming and safe haven for local writers from one end of the spectrum to the other. Yes, whether you write short stories, novels, memoirs, creative non-fiction, poetry, romance, sci-fi, fantasy, or anything else, there is a place for you in London's warm literary embrace. And this anthology, *Out of the Woods*, captures and celebrates the full diversity of London's writers. Whatever your reading preferences may be, there is something—likely many things—for you in this collection.

For many of these London writers, this anthology will be their first time being published—and that's a big deal. Many aspiring writers labour for years honing their craft, shaping their stories, submitting them for publication, and as often as not, collecting rejection letters. It's the lot of every writer. So, to see their stories or poems or essays in this fine anthology, to hold the book in their hands, well, it's a memorable and important moment. It's validation of a sort for the time spent pen to paper and finger to keyboard.

But more importantly, not only are these excellent writers now published, but they will be read. And isn't that ultimately the goal? Writers should be read.

The range of pieces in this anthology reflects not only the diversity of the contributing writers and their city, but also the range of readers who will find this collection, by turns, satisfying, surprising, moving, and enlightening. I admire the writers whose work you'll find between these covers. I like to think I know a thing or two about the perseverance, discipline, desire, and talent required to conceive, write, edit, polish, and submit one's writing for public scrutiny and critique. It's not easy. It's never been easy. But these thirty-five writers have surmounted the obstacles life just seems to throw in the paths of aspiring and established writers alike. Undaunted, they have confronted the blank page or the blinking, taunting cursor, and created worthy works of art that have earned their rightful places in this anthology. And they've done it not just to satisfy a deep desire—sometimes a deep need—to tell stories, but also so that you, dear reader, can join them on the journey and perhaps be moved by it or even changed by it. That is the hope and the power of storytelling.

Now, many of you will have a reading preference. Perhaps some of you only read fiction, or creative nonfiction, or poetry. I understand that. For every biography I read, I probably read six or seven novels. But let me make a suggestion—one that I honoured before writing this. Despite any reading predilections you may have, I encourage you to cast off those shackles and read the entire collection. I'm confident you won't regret broadening your literary horizons and acquainting yourself with other forms of literature that you may not often approach. For me, poetry is my writerly Achilles heel. Sometimes when I read poetry, I struggle to find the meaning the poet has so artfully and thoughtfully conveyed in the lines. I confess it sometimes leaves me feeling inadequate, or worse, that poetry is not for me. Conscious of this shortfall in my writerly life, I've been trying to break through that reluctance and even intimidation that poetry sometimes confers. In the course of my writing life, I've met and befriended a number of poets. So, I've begun reading and enjoying their poems. I also have a hefty tome on my bookshelf entitled *World Poetry: An Anthology of verse from Antiquity to our Time*—an ambitious title to be sure. I dip into it regularly now and am feeling more comfortable with this literary form. In fact, I'm enjoying them. I'm better for them. Yes, that big book, *World Poetry*, is helping to ease me into the poetry world. Similarly, the powerful and accomplished poems in *Out of the Woods* have pushed me further down the road towards a rapprochement—a détente, of sorts—with poetry. It might just do the same for you.

So, please, start at the beginning of *Out of the Woods*, and read your way through it—fiction, nonfiction, poetry. These gifted writers have created art for themselves, but also for you. Reading this anthology honours their art—but not as an act of charity or obligation. Rather, when you've finished reading the last piece, I think you'll agree that you've gained more than you've given—that time-honoured covenant between writer and reader.

This anthology celebrates the writers of London, and so do I. They pass you on the street, unnoticed. They may be serving your meal at a local restaurant, or fixing your car, or doing your taxes. London writers, like most other Canadian writers, live lives not unlike your own. Except, late at night, while others sleep, they are wrestling with words, polishing phrases, and crafting sentences, to create stories. You'll find their diverse and worthy art right here in *Out of the Woods*. Then you will celebrate their art, too.

A Note from the Editor

HEATHER GODDEN

Working on this anthology of London, Ontario writers has been both a pleasure and a privilege. I've been genuinely impressed by the calibre of writing throughout. Many of these pieces would be right at home in well-regarded literary journals, which speaks to the depth of talent in our local writing community.

The challenge of maintaining cohesion across multiple genres while honouring each author's distinct voice proved to be a delicate balancing act. Fiction, poetry and nonfiction each brought their own considerations, yet the pieces flow together remarkably well.

While there wasn't a developmental editing phase, some pieces benefited from subtle adjustments that helped nudge them toward greatness. These moments of collaboration were particularly satisfying.

It's been an honour to work with these talented writers from the London area! The collection you're about to read showcases a remarkable range of perspectives and styles, all connected by a shared geography and commitment to craft.

Out of the Woods – Onto the Page

A MESSAGE FROM THE ANTHOLOGY COMMITTEE

Our inaugural anthology, *Out of the Woods: Voices from the Forest City*, would not have been possible without the participation of the members of the London Writers Society (LWS) who bravely submitted their poems and short stories. Throughout our journey to publication, the excitement and encouragement from LWS members was palpable and kept us motivated. We are proud that the works of thirty-five LWS members are published in this collection.

ABOUT THE ANTHOLOGY COMMITTEE

The idea of an anthology was bounced around for years until 2023 when Ron Cougler, the LWS President at that time, set the plan in motion. He brought together what would become the Anthology Committee—affectionately known as the A-Team—consisting of Donna Costa, Anne Kay, Brenda Martin and Martha Morrison. What started with a seed of an idea, grew into a forest of literary voices.

Astrologically, the four team members are all air signs—the signs of the Zodiac that represent communication—a fun fact that explains our ability to work seamlessly together. We jelled instantly and as we worked behind the scenes to bring this project 'out of the woods' and onto the page, an added bonus was that each of us brought different skills to the project.

With an MFA in creative writing, publishing credits in various anthologies, and a divine sense of choreography that always keeps her several steps ahead, Martha Morrison was a natural choice to serve as the chair of the committee, our effervescent guiding compass. When she started this project, her children were seven months and two years old. We thank Martha's husband and extended family for their support, so vital when a mother works in a position of leadership. (The committee only had to witness one diaper change on Zoom!)

Donna Costa, who has multiple publishing credits, brought to the team her years of administration experience and her profound capacity to maintain grace under fire. As our fiscal manager, she took the lead on the grant application and financial accountability, was a firm contract negotiator and all-round i-dotter and t-crosser, all while juggling her new role as President of the Society. And she still made time to write another book!

Anne Kay came to the committee having recently published her debut historical fiction novel, *The Salt Man*. Her experience with the publishing and promotion process, her extensive background in corporate communications, and her keen eye for detail were integral to the success of the project. As the only committee member who chose not to submit to the anthology, Anne recused herself from meetings for a number of months to serve on the panel of first reader judges.

Backed by decades of creative experience, Brenda Martin was the brains behind the title of the anthology which she casually mentioned during a meeting. It was so perfect, we called her 'Brilliant Brenda' from that moment on. She designed the cover art, posters, sponsorship package, branding, plus so much more, and still managed to keep everything (and us) organized! She also serves as Vice-President for the LWS and works full time.

ACKNOWLEDGEMENTS

We wish to thank the LWS members for trusting us, the Anthology Committee, with this project. And our thanks to the members who volunteered their time and energy, and to those who kindly supported us financially.

To fund the project, we applied for grants and sought sponsorships from our members and local businesses. We are grateful to the London Arts Council and the City of London who demonstrated their belief in this project by awarding us a *Community Arts Investment Program* grant. We must also thank our community for its overwhelming support, and we invite you to look in the back of the book, where you will find a list of the 'literary champions' who opened their hearts and wallets with sponsorships and donations.

There were so many who worked tirelessly both behind the scenes and at public-facing events to bring this collection to fruition. We extend our heartfelt gratitude to:

- Chrissy Hobbs at Indie Publishing Group for generously donating her time and talent to design the interior of the book, prepare the document for publication, and assist us with the publishing process.

- Our tech guru, Marco Muzzi of Wallace & Moody, who created the anthology page on the LWS website, and made countless changes, updates, and additions, all with unflagging cheerfulness.

- Rebecca Hamilton for her social media expertise and promotion.

- Terry Fallis for writing his thoughtful foreword and for stepping up once again to support another LWS project.

- Heather Godden for patiently nurturing the writers through every step of the editing process.

- The esteemed author and publisher Douglas Gibson for taking time to read and provide a review of the anthology.

- Donna Costa for hosting writing sessions at her home, creating a space for community and encouraging camaraderie.

- Our workshop facilitators—Penn Kemp for poetry, Adelle Purdham for nonfiction, and Meg Howald for fiction—whose guidance inspired entrants, elevating their work.

- Members of the established LWS critique group for offering their time as beta-readers for many pieces before they were submitted.

- Justine Dowsett, Publisher at Mirror World Publishing, who freely offered advice about building and publishing an anthology.

- The LWS Executive team and members of the Board of Directors for their unwavering support.

Very special thanks to our volunteer panel of first reader judges—Andreas Connel-Gripp, Barbara Haworth-Attard, Anne Kay, Margaret Whitley, and Kym Wolfe—who rose to the challenge to provide fair and measured scoring of all entries to produce the longlist. And to our finalist judge, Emma Donoghue, who thoughtfully selected every story and poem in this collection.

And finally, to our readers, thank you for purchasing a copy of our inaugural anthology and for 'reading local'. As you turn the pages, you will hear the diverse voices of the Forest City and beyond. And in so doing, perhaps you will catch a glimpse of yourself somewhere in the woods, for these are *our stories*, created by *our neighbours*, written for *our community*.

Together, we have all made this project possible. Thank you!

LWS Anthology Committee:

Martha Morrison (Chair),
Donna Costa, Anne Kay, and Brenda Martin

Nancy Abra
J.R. Boudreau
Charlotte H. Broadfoot
Laurie Browne
Krista Carson
Trudy Cloudt
Donna Costa
Emily De Angelis
Michael Ross Dolan
C.J. Frederick
Bess Hamilton
Stacie Hanson
Catherine Heighway
V. Gregory Houlton
Mackenzie Howson
Eleanor Huber
Barbara Johnson
Mari Johnson
Caroline Kaiser
Diane Kirby
Christine Langlois
Bruce Lord
Adam Love
Brenda Martin
Mary Lou McRae
Dominique Millette
Martha Morrison
J. Edward Orchard
Janice Phillips
Jayn Reed
Stephanie Reisler
Jan Sims
George Allan Tucker
Heather Vanderkam
Laura Wythe

OUT
OF THE
WOODS

VOICES FROM THE FOREST CITY

AN ANTHOLOGY OF
SHORT STORIES & POEMS
BY MEMBERS OF THE
LONDON WRITERS SOCIETY

SELECTED BY
EMMA DONOGHUE

In One Piece

JAYN REED

THE WORKMEN ARE in Bay 2 today. They are an amusing trio, grinning under their masks and talking like old friends as they work within the empty area. Their chatter and the clunk of machines echo from Bay 2, but whenever they step into the main unit, they fall silent and avoid eye contact.

Management sent an email last week warning us to expect some noise as the ICU goes back to normal capacity. It said we're out of the woods now and that it's safe to go back to how things were before. I'm not sure I believe them, considering how recently Omicron kicked our butt. They promised it would cause as little disruption as possible, but they *would* say that, since they have no idea what actually happens on the front line.

Hitting the brake pedal on the hospital bed as we glide into place, I thank the PSW for his assistance. Manoeuvring myself around, I begin exchanging the travel monitor for its permanent counterpart in the room, watching as the screen lights up with data. The short journey down the hall has dropped my patient's blood pressure and, wordlessly, I increase one of his infusions.

Muscle memory takes over as I reach over my patient's

shoulder to straighten his chest leads and detangle the IV lines. The respiratory therapist mirrors my moves, having swapped the portable ventilator for the static one. A colleague wipes down both machines as I systematically move the IV pumps onto the retractable arm and push the empty pole away.

"I'll do your numbers," a masked figure across the central space announces, and I call out my thanks.

I'm the last to arrive in the cubicle, having spent the last forty-five minutes disconnecting Leonardo—one of our continuous renal replacement machines, which each bear the name of a Ninja Turtles character. It is the team's hope that my patient is strong enough to receive hemodialysis again, a situation we've tried twice before without success.

As the transfer equipment is sent back to the storage room, I run through a summary of my patient for my new bay-mates before scooting over to the medication room. Exiting into the main hallway, I watch a blond workman from behind my shield as he helps place the Perspex door on a large stretcher and feel the same sense of foreboding as two years ago.

The pandemic response started with those doors, rapidly transforming my workplace of more than a decade into something unfamiliar and scary. My comfort zone stood just out of reach as I was forced to focus on the usual responsibilities while mentoring those who joined us from the medical floor. While their colleagues stayed to help the rapidly increasing COVID cases upstairs, these brave volunteers came to save us from Italy and New York's fate.

I saw how their eyes widened at the beeping machines, searching for reassurance in the alien world into which they'd ventured. The ICU is a place of mystery to most, whether through preference or good fortune, and it takes a strong person to survive here. Back then, my energy levels were high, and we all wanted to show our appreciation to everyone who came to help.

While Canada first locked itself down, taping arrows in the

grocery and Zooming into meetings, I felt the stress along with everyone else. The unit didn't fill up as early as expected, but the uncertainties still held me hostage. Accessing my fluorescent-lit prison through the employee-only entrance, I would display my app's green tick and my badge to those seated behind the screen, then trudge wordlessly through the inner hallways.

I felt blessed that my unit was only one floor up, saving me from a long wait for the elevator before I dropped my food off in the lounge and beeped my way into the secure unit. There I would join my workmates clutching our plastic bags for dear life, as if the two N95 masks per twelve-hour shift would protect us from decimating our families.

Some colleagues moved out of their homes as a precaution, while others avoided hugging their kids. Reminders of the SARS outbreak of '03 became a topic of conversation, and for those of us that missed it, the idea of bringing a silent disease home was new. Suddenly, it felt real, much more than the occasional TB or shingles case ever did.

By the time the summer came and only a few unlucky souls had graced our beds, homemade scrub caps and #IVEGOTYOUR-BACK911 shirts were everywhere—a sign of our growing camaraderie—and the unit was unrecognizable.

We were ready for the onslaught, with every bay having swelled to accommodate six patients instead of the usual four, and the central area in between was cluttered with extra wheeled computers and poles littered with multiple IV pumps, affectionately known as Trees.

At a time when social distancing became a thing, I remember being physically closer to my colleagues than ever. To say it was claustrophobic would be pretty accurate, and that was before the washable PPE arrived.

Brought in as a replacement for the disposable ones that ran out far too quickly, these were threadbare yellow versions of the backless gowns our patients wore. Unlike those ass-parading ones, these came in large dumpsters that violated the fire exit codes for the sake of outbreak avoidance.

The nurses' lounge was the only space available to breathe. Since there were no visitors allowed, our manager utilized the abandoned waiting room as a secondary break space, allowing us to stretch out in masked silence while abiding by the rules. Back then, I was naively hoping that the changes were short-term, thinking it an overreaction much like the Ebola training we did in 2019. That particular situation didn't come to anything, but the hazmat suits eventually came in handy with the sickest patients during this pandemic.

As I wade through my shift, listening to the almost constant alarms and rhythmic whooshing of the ventilators, I spy our ward clerk helping a handful of lost-looking relatives. Meanwhile, my patient slowly deteriorates. He desperately needs a kidney transplant but is too sick now, even if he was higher up on the waitlist. For now, all we can do is buy him time and try to reverse the multi-organ failure that has taken hold. He has maxed out all his meds and even though we started another IV, I get ready to reattach Leonardo.

His tearful relatives arrive, and we hold a family meeting to discuss the next steps. It is in the boardroom, with everyone spread out around the large table that dominates the space. I sit next to his wife, smiling gently with my eyes, thankful for this morsel of change. It's a relief to see visitors in the unit again, after their long absence during this nightmare.

No one had visitors, not even those actively dying. Instead, we would use FaceTime, holding the tablet above the unconscious face while the family crowded around their own device and cried on the other side of the city or province. I remember how my arms would ache keeping it at just the right angle so they could speak and send their love and prayers. Dressed in several layers of PPE, I would smile when I spoke even though no one, not even my colleagues, recognized my features. We began identifying each other only by our muffled comments.

We started to get swamped with patients near the end of the first year and stayed that way for most of the second. My memory of 2021 is mostly absent, missing in a flurry of activity that was too much to process. All I know is that most of my shifts were a haze of days and nights sweating under my layers, as my nose slowly decayed from the N95 masks and my energy waned.

The staff-only entrance became a kind of bubble one entered, glancing at the world through social media and the unwashed windows that were hiding behind the overloaded shelves. We missed the clapping, although the painted rocks left along the side of the path boosted spirits as they grew in abundance.

Quiet shifts had become but a memory, and the unit managers stopped dancing on TikTok, leaving only dark humour and anxiety behind. There were no volunteers anymore, compassionate folk who used to share a joke or help calm jittery relatives.

Instead, we had The Island, which in another lifetime had been the recovery area for day surgery. It became the overflow or surge area when the unit was above capacity. We first opened it in October 2020, and it was a disaster. The cardiac monitors they had didn't link to the ICU, and the lack of medical support when things went sideways meant that in the end, only the most stable patients could go there.

My replacement arrives, sighing as his eyes take in the extra machines and pumps. The patient is worse this evening than when my colleague left this morning, treading achingly close to needing ECMO—the heart and lung machine that is an all-too-familiar Hail Mary strategy of late. His family has just left after an afternoon of tears and compassion, a frequent theme in a typical shift.

I update all key information, discussing how things deteriorated and the tentative plans for the next few hours. It is my swan song until later this week. The coded information flows from me—familiar words and phrases that lately carry more bite than ever. I am tired, burnt out and slightly broken, but by Saturday morning at 6:45 a.m., I will be back to do it all again.

Rolling my shoulders back, I turn to collect my backpack from the corner and silently wish my dying patient good luck. Spotting the hi-vis workers' cart stowed next to Bay 3, I wonder if the same energetic crew from today will be back tomorrow. I resented their presence this morning, but tonight they give me hope that the world's usual mayhem might return after all.

The effects of this pandemic are decreasing their hold on me now, no longer forcing me to see catastrophes in every little thing. My insomnia is improving, as are the dreams, but the fight-or-flight instinct that kicks in whenever I hear an alarm persists.

The Employee Assistance Program tells me to talk about my experiences, but when I try, a lump in my throat silences the first words and tears wash away the rest. I've always been like that, struggling to keep myself together as I express my feelings. It makes people think I am upset when all I'm doing is speaking from my heart. My husband gets it, thankfully, but sometimes I just want to let it out without the dehydration factor.

I've taken to writing, allowing the words to flow unedited and unread. They live in the drawer in our bedroom. It was the only new skill I picked up during lockdown, lacking the bandwidth on my days off to do anything else.

There is no sourdough bread lurking in my freezer, and I didn't learn to knit. There was no cabin fever for me; instead, I savoured the quiet. The absence of machines playing their threatening tones resuscitated my mind, preserved my sanity and recharged my fortitude until another day off was earned.

The world is going back to normal proceedings with fervour, but I intend to navigate this new normal carefully. Buried deep under all the angst, I am happy to have survived and grateful for the opportunity to help those less fortunate. I realize I am not alone in this—someday, our shared rite of passage will make for great stories.

As one of the lucky ones, I do not dwell on how my kids missed out on graduation or a regular high school life. Although I miss watching medical dramas, I have sports to relax me rather than the shows that remind me of my life's work. The phrase "self-care" may be new and woke, but it has become a small part of my toolbox in a world that exists differently now.

As I pull into my driveway, I see the curtains still open. It is dusk and my husband is lit up in the glare of the kitchen. He's standing by the stove as he prepares a late evening meal to coincide with the end of my shift, and my stomach gives an appreciative roll. Closer, my son's feet are resting on the coffee table just beyond the bay window, his socks bearing holes that expand as he wiggles his toes. His headphones are on, most likely playing his current audiobook as he relaxes next to his older brother who's blond, frowning head is bent over his laptop. University notes are scattered around him, and he is chewing the inside of his cheek as he studies the screen.

This is my family, the reason for everything. They are why I've endured leaving the safety of this home to try to sustain others amid a tide of uncertainty. As the expected lump forms and my eyes sting, I smile and fumble for my keys, content to unwind until Saturday beckons.

I am home.

Natus Mortuus

BRENDA MARTIN

The moon reversed her orbit the day you were not born.
I felt her axis tilt and shift, unexpected,
without a whisper of breath, breath you would not take.
A contraction—a pregnant plenilune pull—
shimmering iridescent and full,
spiralled retrograde.

Captive in the constant choreography of time and tide,
I recall the kicks and jabs of the you that was,
an ephemeral being, never to love, to laugh, to cry. Never.
In grieving dreams, I conjure you, your *what would be,*
and to the moon, from perigee to apogee,
I moan and howl.

Goddess Selene laboured to create a palingenesis, in vain.
Your premature arrival a departure,
a diminutive collision of nativity and mortality.
Bereft, my witness—my glimmering Greek confidante—
and I—a crescent writhing and wracked with want—
waxed and mourned.

Enlisted by his sister to abort this danse macabre,
Helios failed in his fruitless quest to reset time,
to halt the relentless ebb and flow, to wax gibbous again.
Wrought with despair—impotent sun, moon luminous, and me
pale and waning—in unison, we three
keened and prayed

to Gaia, to Jehovah, to *every* god. To every star.
We prayed to invoke a recalibration, a new trajectory
by circumgyration, an intervention divine. We prayed
'til our anguished orisons aligned, exposing the futility of denial
and, cast in the twilight of totality, the umbral pall
eclipsed all hope.

Megatheria

J.R. BOUDREAU

W E NEEDED SOMEONE to keep watch for the wardens, so we talked Valerie into driving us in my car. Her golden hair and hoop earrings swayed with the turns, and the night fog hovered above the ditches as she guided the two-door Dodge along the road. Nobody had risked the action at the headwaters of the Thames.

Due to careful marriages and parenthood, we only slip into each other's lives the odd year now, but in those days, we lived according to our whims, not our means. We'd aim for the moon: a few beers here, a shot of something there, a buffet of magic mushrooms for dessert. Ogilvy, Val's half-brother, had even proposed a fish fry for breakfast, since his new bride worked the night shift, and because Ed and Val were sticking it out until Monday. Ed was my cousin, a former Argo with a head like a tombstone. He and Valerie lived in a suburb in Vaughan, right next to Wonderland, rollercoasters for lullabies.

In the backseat, I watched Val's soft profile in oncoming headlights. Ed caught and then disrupted me by wondering, "What's with the deer around here anyway?"

"They've bin roamin' into town more and more," said Ogilvy, riding shotgun beneath an earnest mullet. "Even in daylight, one'll bolt out an alley fer a run down the pavement."

"An old lady got bowled over in front of me and Ed yesterday," Valerie said. "Broke her hip."

"I heard that'll kill you," I injected without thinking.

"Who'd you hear that from?"

"Well, studies show."

Valerie parked at the end of the bridge to unload us and then sped off. She'd go back and forth for a kilometre, the river in the middle, so that nobody would notice the green Dodge parked under the lights. We started toward a limited footpath. Ogilvy carried a net in one hand and in the other, a rod with a small steel hook moulded to its tip. Just a flask in his back pocket, Ed was barehanded, claiming he'd feel 'em and grab 'em. A pitchfork I'd found in one of the old sheds rested across my forearm. Ed hadn't thought of that.

Brave in the valley, we steadied ourselves against the cedars, the tight branches breaking against our thighs and spanking us. Many of the higher tops were already snapped off, an anomaly of the area supposedly noted by that logging crew that disappeared near here. Red oak leaves layered the earth and gave eagerly beneath our boots as we reached the water.

Then Ogilvy cried out, "Oh, no, *no*, I didn't!" and fell back through a fence of cattails. Soaked, but on his feet again in an instant, he explained, "Just stepped on a feckin snapper! Thought it was a rock."

As was mine and Ogilvy's usual practice, we pressed our jeaned knees into the cold river and waded slow as driftwood into the midst of the fish. The waterway groaned and gobbled and tried to swallow us or else spit us out. On both edges, those thick cattails moved in course and clunked together menacingly while we waited for the salmon to settle, fresh deposits in a doomed restocking effort.

Before long, Ed mumbled, "Got one."

Its belly crackled silver under the moonlight.

"Beginner's luck," I said.

"That's life."

Stabbing the water, I poached another from the sanctuary, and from the MNR, and pitched it off the tines onto the bank with two or three more. Their mouths gasped for the same oxygen that surrounded them, flopping and wringing the power out of their own bodies. I would've gutted one that evening, given the chance, and eaten it with a conscience clear as whiskey before it's barrelled.

Instead, the stench of a waterdog overtook me. It reminded me of the big Newfie Ed had when we were kids, a dog that elected to roll in cow dung and nap in puddles, gladly logging the stink in his fur. Just as fleetingly, the odour passed. If the branches hadn't risen and fallen in my periphery, I wouldn't have noticed the figure moving in the shadows. Because of the rapids near the bridge, you couldn't hear it, but we saw the wide, momentary splash in the river, and then sudden beams of light were flung from silhouettes above and scattered across the ripples. Two cars were parked up there now. One was green. The other flashed red and blue.

"Goddamnit," said Ogilvy.

He went for the far riverbank and jogged into the dark. More flashlights hacked through the black foliage and landed on Ed, who laid down and drifted off with the current. Boots moved in the bushes after him, back toward the bridge.

"Good luck!" I called as I planted the pitchfork in the bank, and Ed's laugh came back. I fought upstream, dipping now and then beneath the inky water. It concealed me from the law.

I broke out onto a gravel road on the other side of the woods. A body trudged toward me through the fog, casting a beam to and fro.

Valerie finally emerged. In a leather jacket leaking river water, her checkered shirt was suctioned to her breasts and tucked into jeans that rode up to her belly button.

"It's foggy as hell," I said, and she jolted.

"They were waiting for us!" she told me, lips thinning into a magnificent smile. Her hair was tied back and her smooth, broad face speckled with mud. She smelled of cold dirt. "They towed your car. Tried to haul me in, too, but I grabbed the torch and dove over."

I couldn't help but laugh. Ogilvy was already in a cell, or on his way to one. And when the cops searched the trunk and found walleye eggs from a couple weekends prior, out in Byron, I'd get a two-thousand-dollar fine, and the car itself would be auctioned off in exchange for not a penny. But at the time, I was walking through the woods beside Valerie, and I laughed.

I asked her, "How's Ed treating you?"

"Good," she said, watching the ground.

"Things haven't fallen apart yet?"

"Tom."

"What?"

"*You're* the one who ended it."

"Well, I didn't know he was with you, too."

"He got over it."

"Then I'll get over it."

"That'll be the day," she laughed.

"Didn't we have dreams, Val?"

"They died, Tom. That's what dreams do."

What else can you call them but dead dreams, those foolish memories of smoking a morning jay in the windy park? Her body on mine, in the deckchair at a rented cottage, her breath damp and hot, eyes so bright and blue that God himself must've hole-punched the summer sky to provide them? All of this publicly cancelled when she moved away to take a situation with Gay Lea, selecting Ed to go with her. Back then, these memories ate up any ambition in me.

The scent of rotting leaves misted the wind. Also on the breeze rode the echo of a high, hollow wail.

Valerie asked, "What the hell was that?"

They knew their path, but they moved jerkily through the reeds toward one another. Speaking first in a pleading, sing-song language, the pair halted naked in a grove of gibbous moonlight, muscled and anxious. Then they roared, charged, collided with a clatter, and grappled in low combat.

"Centaurs…" I muttered.

"*What?*" asked Valerie in a tone of shame and incredulity. "How many mushrooms did you *eat,* Tom? They're *deer*!"

"Jesus Christ," I said, appalled.

Spotting us, the stags froze. They stared with eyes dark, antlers tangled and necks knotted. We proceeded slowly along the dirt road until we'd passed beyond the bushline and out of view.

"Something's got 'em spooked," I said.

Eventually, Valerie asked, "You remember those loggers that got lost out here in '67?"

"Vanished, eh? And then those fellas came to town to make a documentary about whatever became of 'em."

Those tall, bald Germans had rented out the high school gym and projected their film at two bucks a head the following summer. A shaky home video of something dark and plodding behind the trees along the river, its eyes reflecting in the declining light. The noise of the filmmakers arguing in their native speak dominated the whole affair, and their horses neighed frantically in the background. A prank, we figured, or a big bear posturing on its hind legs.

Valerie said, "Some still claim to see it every few years, Ogilvy told me. Says it's been snarling through these bogs longer than we been breathing." She held the flashlight under her chin and hissed, mimicking her half-brother's heavy inflection: "*It's somethin older than these trees, Tommy, somethin that regards us as we do the lesser creatures, the fish or the fowl. 'As above, so below,' ain't that the maxim?*"

I could feel my brows, stretched and tense, somewhere high on my forehead. My eyes were lidless and dry. I accepted that the night wasn't full of nothing, after all, and I watched the flashlight beam illuminate the dirt road before us, its glow only knowing so much of the path at a time. Beyond its weaponry, there was an endless wilderness where not even light dared to go. That same blackness swarmed up behind us, and would devour us automatically if we stopped walking. Then Valerie tickled my ear and I jumped. She cackled until she was breathless.

A miraculous, orange three-wheeler rolled up slow, stinking of fumes, its tires munching the gravel. Ed was its driver. His sweater fluttered in the breeze and distorted into a thicket of fiddleheads.

"You survived!" said Valerie.

"Wandered upon somebody's cabin, but nobody was home."

"So you stole their three-wheeler?" I asked.

"The door was wide open. Like they'd run out."

"So you stole the three-wheeler."

Valerie kissed his cheek. "Good job, babe. God, there must be a bathroom around here," she said, then hopped over some brambles and ducked into the trees to squat and piss relief.

As she crashed away, Ed asked bluntly, "You still love her?"

"Oh, fuck off."

"I know," he said. "Loving how she makes you feel, being the one to make her laugh, laying claim to her beauty. Loving yourself, really, I guess. She ain't gonna complete you, Tommy. We're complete as we're gonna get."

The years reduced to a moment of silent, familial awkwardness as he nodded along with his own mind. Then Ed unpocketed his flask and passed it to me. I felt its weight, raised it to him, and slugged half the scotch in one go. I returned it, and he drained what remained. Locking eyes at last, we instantly began to belt a Stan Rogers tune, rocking arm-in-arm against the three-wheeler, the way we'd done at Ogilvy's buck and doe the past summer.

Then Valerie exploded from the treeline without the flashlight, still zipping up her jeans. She shouted, "The *cops,* you idiots!"

We turned to discover two officers spectating from either side of a parked cruiser, doors ajar. One began toward us, his palms lifted to the stars in a calming sign.

"Poaching doesn't pay, boys, poaching doesn't pay…" he intoned.

There was a brief charge of energy from Ed, though he suppressed it and allowed himself to be folded into the backseat like an oversized taxidermy. But as the door closed and the cop turned to me, the opposite door popped open and Ed's body plunged to the dirt with a grunt. The other officer spun at the sound and started a malicious sprint toward Ed, circling the front of the car. Then, from several feet away, he pulled his legs up and dropkicked the backdoor just as Ed rolled clear of its path.

"*You tried to decapitate me!*" he shouted, laughing in disbelief.

A gallant man and true, Ed rolled along the gravel, to his knees, then his feet, and somehow darted large and foxlike down the road as both cops hounded after.

I told Valerie, "Let's go then, you and me."

She hugged my back as I ignited the three-wheeler and clenched my fist. We ripped down the dirt road. Eventually, I veered right, and we plunged into the bushes and down a tight path that would, I hoped, vein toward society.

I told the wind, "Ed's a good guy."

"He is," said Valerie.

"He don't love you like I love you," I admitted.

She shrugged against me. "You're an Aries. Too melancholic.

And I need someone more sanguine, Tom. It's not my job to complete you."

"I keep hearing that."

We took a lunar run through the forest and the three-wheeler manoeuvred its way over a briar patch. We ducked beneath the long and tilted trees, dead and bare and interlaced with living others—to open upon another meadow, confronted by the remains of some sort of absolute cathedral. The robins and owls were fluting and fussing in the trees around us.

"This," said Valerie, "gives me the holy fuckin creeps."

Its walls had been charred by flames and shaved by time, reduced to its foundations. I dismounted the three-wheeler and wandered between the cobwebbed and lopped-off pillars. The building's original outline was obvious: a triangular opening widened into a great hall that ended in an isosceles antechamber. Stone columns were at each angle and midpoint.

Her nose blushed from the wind, Valerie whispered, "*Tom…*"

Reverent and sudden, the birds quit their sounding. The forest became a loose tarp over a commotion that rippled along the branches and leaves like a current.

Valerie shrieked, terror from some part of the brain that predates the capacity for language, an animal signal for emergency. I glanced at her and tracked her panicked sight to the thick of the timber. Tall and motionless beech trunks. Gliding limbs of willow. I must've stared at it, unaware, for five seconds solid. But something was panting primal in the fog, and I inhaled the musty reek of beast. Then, scraping the high branches, a humanoid form slouched forward from beyond the common world. It unleashed an overwhelming, primordial howl. I rushed back to Valerie and we blew down a labyrinth of paths as fast as the three-wheeler would allow. It quaked and begged against the lumpy ground while screams rebounded around us.

I don't say I saw anything properly. And when I see Valerie, she never speaks of it, though she still teases me in front of Ed and Ogilvy for mistaking the deer that night. Yet when the autumn sun falls in the countryside, or if I close my eyes in the woods, there lingers a ready glimpse of the thing. A furry flash of claws and teeth. Amber eyes reflective as a predator's. We saw something. It saw us.

That night, though, we were terrified but alive. We made it back to charted terrain, and as we cruised through the dark toward a half-remembered boundary, I had to slow to basically nothing. Valerie pinched my waist in fear.

"There's a fence around here somewhere," I explained, but then the three-wheeler surrendered into a lower mode. It revved and pulsed without moving. I gunned it again, but to no luck.

"Come *on*," Valerie said.

"I'm giving it all the gas and it's not moving!" I shouted.

Valerie stood up behind me. She pressed her hips into my back, squished my chest into the handlebars with her torso, and leaned over my shoulder. Her fingertips trickled down chain links as the fence bent against the three-wheeler. All along, it had been right there in front of us.

Heart's Desire

BESS HAMILTON

T HE COMING HERE was hard. He said, *It will be worth it, Mary. Don't fret on it.* Because what was there behind us? *Nothing*, he said. *Just rocks and land that don't belong to us.* And I would add, under my breath, *Nothing but home. Nothing but our families. Nothing but our hearts.*

My heart shattered into pieces the day we boarded the boat. When our youngest girl died of the flux on the way over, I sent a piece of my heart into the sea with my girl. All along our journey, I left shards of my broken heart along my path like the children in the story do to mark their path to home.

The first year was hard. The lord's big words amounted to not much. We didn't come to a utopia. We got the land he promised. But what of it? What wasn't marsh was full of trees we had to clear ourselves. The lord hadn't said there were already people here who called this land their home and wanted none of us. They'd warned the men back and said not to cut the trees or something terrible would fall upon us. Just as my granny had said a wise farmer would leave a tree for the forest folk to harbour in. But none listened and the trees came down, leaving the land naked, with stumps sticking out of the snow like broken teeth.

Our first months were spent in tents and then shivering in log huts when the winter came. So many of our neighbours died. I would look to the east and think of home all through that long winter. Perhaps it wasn't Christian of me to sorrow so. I'd lay awake at night, listening to my man snoring beside me and wishing I'd never tied myself to him.

He said, *Mary, don't take on so. This is our home now. Our children will be free. They won't see their labour go to fill a lord's pockets, to be wasted on sport and women.* And that was true. But it wasn't enough for me.

He said, *Mary, you should be happy with the new bairn. She is the spit of her sister, the one we lost. She was beautiful and so like her sister. So very like, indeed.*

I never said much in reply. The other women thought me cold, but I never turned a stranger from our door. Nor did I refuse a neighbour any help. It was just the pieces of my heart stuck in my throat, blocking my words. My heart pieces kept the anguish from bursting out. If it ever did, I'd never be able to force it back inside again.

Time moved forward, like a current pulls a boat along, dragging us further and further from our past life. Everyone worked together to clear the trees, drain the marsh, plant the crops. Our house grew a little more comfortable with every harvest. My children, the ones who survived the coming and the ones born here, thought of this place as home. He said, *Look at these fine Canadians we're raising.* And they were so fine. They were strong and handsome and smart. But they'd have been as fine, no, they'd have been finer at home. I could have loved them more there, unafraid of losing them to this new place. Because no one stayed still. They always looked to somewhere else, another promised land.

My husband brought me seeds from the city. *For flowers,* he said. *You can have some beauty to look upon as you work. You always did like flowers, I recall.* My mother had flowers around her cottage, even if others thought it foolish to spend time tending things that were neither food nor medicine. There were flowers here, in the woods and the cleared places. But they were strangers to me. He'd brought old friends with familiar names. My daughters and I sowed the seeds where I'd see the blooms from my kitchen window. He said, *They're to gladden your heart. Tell me how to gladden your heart.* But I couldn't say, *Take me home,* because that would be impossible. He loved it here, as did my children.

When one of my fine Canadian sons died, the flowers were beautiful around him in his coffin. A piece of my heart went into the ground with him, just as I'd left a piece in the sea with his sister.

My girls pressed or dried my flowers, so I'd have them to look at through the long, dark winters. In those dark days, I'd think of the seeds sleeping beneath the ground, waiting for spring just as I did. Did they ever think of their homeland? Or were they content to grow wherever they were planted?

The old woman from the cottage down the lane would come begging for a few flowers every summer. I never asked what she did with them. They were poor, her family. Her boys, men, really, didn't work as hard as other men here. And she was a strange one, always muttering to herself. Many said she often walked into the long woods to talk to the Devil. They said the lord had packed her off his land for some evil, some curse she'd hissed out at him once when their paths had crossed.

One day, she looked at me with her one sharp eye. Her other eye was as smoothly white as a piece of quartz worn by tumbling about in a river. People said her white eye saw things beyond most men's ken. Her sharp eye was young and like a bird's eye, always roving, dark and glittering. With that eye she surely saw enough.

She said, *I can get you what you desire most.* My tattered heart stopped in my chest. *But what is the cost?* I asked her. Because I understood, caught in the dual gaze of her sharp eye and milky eye, the stories were true.

She said, *It would only cost your husband's joy. And one of your bonny daughters.* God help me, I agreed to the bargain. She laughed at my firm yes and she said, *I only mean for one of my sons to marry one of your daughters.* She said, *You were ready to give one up entirely.* I replied, *I have already given two. One to the sea. One to this land.* What was another?

My husband's trials began that very day. Indeed, our whole family was bedevilled.

Stones came like bullets through the windows at all times. Yet none of us were ever struck. Still, my eldest daughter said, *I cannot live here, always waiting to be killed.* When the old lady's son came and asked to marry her, my daughter, who'd never spoke a word to him before, said yes and was gone. They went north, through the long woods, moving to a place long settled and less wild.

Soon after, the fires started. Little fires sprang up like weeds. They left charred marks through our house and in our gardens and fields. He said, *We need to leave this cursed place.* My heart leaped. But he only meant to go to another house in the village. My eldest son married and left us to our troubles. Another daughter left to work as a servant in a fine house in the closest port. Although, what was a fine house here would have been nothing more than a plain farmhouse back home.

The fires followed us to the new house my husband and sons built. Tables jumped, dishes flew, animals died. But my husband had enough of moving so he stayed. Our barn burned, though, and then our house, so that we were reduced to tents once more.

Whenever the old woman saw me, she'd wink and tap her nose. *Soon,* she would whisper to me as she took a nosegay of flowers. *Soon, you will have your heart's desire.*

Men, though, love to solve a problem when the best solution would be to leave, to quit. No. They want to stay. They want to win. The men of the settlement put their brains to it. My husband couldn't leave it be, although we were shivering in tents and only the littlest children remained with us because they couldn't yet marry or take work in other families.

First came the schoolmaster. He nailed up a sign asking evil to be gone from our place. He had read it in a book, he told us. The minister didn't like it, nor did the law. A magistrate came up from the port city and arrested the schoolmaster for taking pay to hunt witches. After several months in jail, he was set free because my son wrote to say the schoolmaster had done it on his own, for no money. The sign caught fire in the night as it was.

The fires popped up all through the summer, growing larger. Each time my husband attempted to rebuild, a fire would consume his work. He said, *We must have done something to earn God's wrath.* I said nothing.

The French folks from the neighbouring settlement, afraid the evil would spread to them, sent their priest to us. He said words in Latin and wrestled mightily with something, but to no purpose. Stones still fell from the sky behind my children and ripped through the tents and the fires yet burned.

Be patient, the old woman said. *You will get your desire.*

Then the doctor said he knew of a girl who could see into the next world. My husband agreed to go with him. He said, *I'll be back soon. I don't want to make deals with witches, but something must be done, or we will have to leave this place.* I said nothing, but I smiled as he walked away.

He was gone a week. In my dreams, I saw him in the woods, beset by wolves. Every night, I watched as the wolves pulled him down and then looked up at me, their snouts dripping blood. One would drop his heart at my feet and sit like a dog, waiting for a reward. Every morning when I woke, I said, *If he doesn't return, I will go home.*

He returned.

He said, *I need a silver bullet. Have you not seen the great dark bird that watches us? The children see it.* I said, *This is foolishness. A silver bullet. How will you get such a thing?*

He took my silver cup and had the blacksmith melt it down and form it into a ball. The cup had been my mother's, and it had belonged to her mother and so on back through the years. It was to have been my oldest daughter's. Of all the things I'd brought with us, other than my children, it was the dearest to me. No jewel could be more precious. Yet, he took it.

When he left with his gun, a final great fire came and took our tent and our cart and our fields. All but my flowers were devoured and left as ashes.

Pain ripped through my chest. *I have shot it,* he said. *Come see,* he cried. *Come see the great bird I've shot. Right through the breast,* he cried.

But I stood amongst my flowers, unable to move for the searing pain, worse than any I had felt. A warm red puddle spread around my feet, soaking the hem of my dress.

Come see, he said, rushing up to me as if he were a young man again. He stopped on the lane, his face white. He dropped the gun, little caring if it should fire by accident. *What happened?* he cried.

I'm going, I said to him. I laughed and laughed as I fell. I had never told the witch in words what I'd wanted. I thought I'd wanted to return home. I'd been so sure. Every day since we'd boarded the boat, I'd yearned for it. But then I knew. I'd really wanted to stop my heart from being torn away piece by piece. The witch had made it so my heart would go all at once.

Edges of Motherhood

HEATHER VANDERKAM

Standing in my dining room wearing a diaper
Matching the diapered newborn strapped to my chest.
When we discussed a fourth
We didn't plan for a pandemic.
My husband kisses us goodbye.
He is essential.
He drives past the edges of our property.
The current confines of our lives.
My envy is palpable.
Standing in my dining room with two children on their computers.
One eagerly engaged, the other upside down in his chair.
Hearing the kindergarten teacher call his name, trying her hardest
To hold his attention within the edges of the screen.
Sitting with him to encourage (plead with) him to focus.
Covering my nursing baby so the class doesn't see my left breast.
Wishing the fresh-faced, childless teacher
Knew how hard I am trying.
Breathe.
The recycled suburb air only partially fills my lungs, with no relief.

The edges of the minimalist white rooms closing in on me.
Moving away from the glare of disapproval radiating from
the screen.
Finding my toddler entrenched in the flashes of her own
handheld device.
Wrapping her in her great-grandmother's quilt.
Her namesake who survived the plague of her generation by
Eating tubers from farmers' fields.
How will I survive?
I find myself lifting the edges of the quilt.
Peek.
Seeing the smile on her face so desperately searching for the smile
on mine.
Isolating myself with my most beautiful creations.
Longing for gratitude.
The edges of my skin barely containing the building anxiety,
Which leaks out as tears streaming onto the quilt—I imagine them
Resting where my grandmothers' tears once fell.
Joined by the drops from the fussy cries of a screaming baby
Still tied to my chest.
All of us seeking connection with something much more than this.
Needing a change, loading them into the family van,
Spacious and reliable: everything my mind is not.
Driving past playgrounds once filled with the sounds of
children playing
My ears yearning for the laughter.
In pursuit of sanctuary.
Arriving to the edges of the forest.
Mother Nature is always open.
Unearthing this foreign familiarity.
The kids run with gusto toward the stream.
All but the baby, who is still strapped to my chest.
Breathe.

Warm damp air encompasses
The outermost edges of my every cell.
My son feels it too,
Upside down without need for correction.
Watching as my toddler steps into the water.
The edges of her chubby feet sparkle in the trickling water.
Bathing in the glow of the sun between the leaves.
Resting deeply in generations of mothers before me
Who have been mothered by the Earth.

Parents

MICHAEL ROSS DOLAN

T HE CHILD WOKE with a cough. Nothing moved in the cabin save for the pale swirls of breath and a few morning motes, caught in thin shafts of light from the window. The cabin had one room, split evenly between bed, cot, kitchen and table. Once more the child coughed, this time with a rough forcefulness that set its thin arms swaying. A deep, earthen groan came from the corner of the room as the father raised himself out of bed and walked over to the cot. He lifted the child, wrapped in a woven nest of blankets, and moved closer to the kitchen stove; the night's fire had faded and it was cold.

"The stove is low," the man said to his wife, who had turned over in bed toward the wall in protest against the sound of his footsteps. When no reply came, the man set down the child and began rummaging through what remained of their woodpile. This disturbance proved sufficient to rouse the mother, who suddenly threw off her blankets and rolled from the bed. Gathering the child in her arms, she stood and waited while the man sorted through a collection of flimsy cuts from the pile. She pressed the back of her hand to the child's forehead.

"What's there won't last much longer," the woman said, "and the fever hasn't changed. We'll need more."

The man rose from his squat by the pile, carrying a small armful of pieces before throwing them into the stove with a shrug. He dusted off his hands and turned to the woman.

"It's enough for breakfast at least, so let's eat. Then I'll go out to cut more."

"Where? You said there's nothing good left around here, it's too green."

"There's some older woods down past the fields, close to that little creek. It's farther than I'd like but I figure there'll be enough in there."

"Your axe sharp enough this time?"

The man grunted in response and sat down at the table. The mother handed him the child, then set about growing the fire and cooking their meal. While she worked, the father studied the child's face, the sallow skin and pale lips. He looked up at the back of his wife as she moved about the kitchen, wanting to speak to her but thinking better of it. It was no use, she worried enough, and she understood the way things were going just as well as he did. There had been nights he had woken to find her out of bed, standing in a dim stream of moonlight from the window and watching over the cot with her hands on its edge, motionless. He was afraid to bring it up with his wife, to admit he had watched her watching. No matter how badly he wanted to console her in those moments, to tell her of his own fears to make her feel less alone, he simply could not bring himself to intrude on her ruminations. It would only add to her troubles, knowing he was no less concerned than her. As he watched her working, he noticed she had begun to develop a slouch in her back.

The meal was served and they ate without a word spoken. Only the occasional snap of the fire or mumble of the child sounded out in the cabin's confines. When he was finished eating, and without clearing his setting, the man stood and moved toward the door, where his coat hung on the wall.

"Bring back as much as you can manage," the woman said without looking at him.

"Winter's breaking," the man mused in reply, "so shouldn't be too long now before we only need it for cooking."

"But the nights are still cold, and we need to keep the place as warm as we can. We've burned more than we planned, not that we had a choice, and until things improve that's not going to change. The snow's gone so less insulation along the walls, and the wind is going to whip through like every year. Until it's summer we'll need plenty more."

The man was silent; he had nothing more to say and he knew better than to raise doubts. He wrangled on his coat, grabbed his axe and a length of rope, and left the cabin. Outside he took a few brisk steps from the door, his head hung low, deep in thought, counting the days and the weeks of fretting, of sickness, of sleeplessness and helplessness and inability. His mind churned and sputtered, guessing at times and possibilities while he started across the tilled plot around the homestead, but as he raised his eyes to check the path, he felt his thoughts recede and dim. Before him, he found a world transformed by the cool touch of night into an expanse of glassy, shimmering crystal—a spring morning, freshly hatched from winter's shell. Where yesterday had been only browns and murky greens there now shone rivers of golden sun-sparkled frost, flowing down and between the rows of earth. The man set out west over the field in the direction of the nearby stream, and as he walked, he felt the early light slowly warm his back through his coat and his trousers, settling along his neck and in his hair like a gentle hand, a comfort. He slowed his pace and inhaled a deep breath as he stretched; the air was still cold enough to sting his lungs. Craning his head backwards, he exhaled a lazy white puff, the only cloud to be seen against the blue sky.

"Looks like I may have overdressed," he said wryly to himself as he resumed his walk. "Hardly need this coat by the time I'm done if this weather keeps up."

But soon the man reached the end of the field and started to track downward toward the water, taking him out of the sun and into the shadow of the slope. Scattered trees began to appear as he followed the stream farther down. From somewhere in the tree-tops above his head there came remote bird calls, gentle trills and chirps whose notes rang together into the likeness of a melody. They brought to his mind an old song he had heard as a boy while working in the field with his father. He could not remember the words, only their rough story, a vague impression of a family watching their son go off to war, but the tune remained in his memory and so he started to hum as he walked deeper into the shade. Ice hid in the cracked crevices and thin seams along the tree bark, and a delicate layer of snow still lay in patches upon the withered blades of grass. Now well out of the sun, he found whatever warmth he had gathered up to that point had abandoned him, and he pulled his coat on tighter.

Mercifully, the copse he had mentioned to his wife soon came into view. As he reached it, he immediately began his search for a suitable tree. The small wood contained a mix of beech, oak, maple, ash and spruce, but the man was disappointed to find few of the trees were worthwhile. Many were simply too small, others still green despite their age and size. Reaching the end of the copse, he curved around the perimeter and looked in at the motley squadron of trunks, some sloped and slouched, others standing at attention. And there, tucked in a corner at the rear of the bunch, stood a dry, weary ash, neither too small nor too large and nearly dead-standing, with only a smattering of optimistic buds sprouting from its upper branch tips.

The man quickly set up at its base. He leaned his axe against the tree, tossed his rope on the ground a few feet away, and slipped on a pair of rough leather gloves he had pulled from his coat pockets.

Then, gathering up the axe in a two-handed grip, he took his stance and began to work. A few rough, cursory strikes were enough to mark his cut before he circled round the trunk a few paces and started again on the new angle. Within a minute he had fallen into a workman's trance as each hearty *thock* echoed through the woods and kept time to his measured swings. Thin beads of sweat soon formed on his neck and brow, freezing his skin as they cooled. When the cut was nearly a quarter way through the trunk he paused, but only long enough to wipe his face and adjust his grip on the axe before setting back to the task at his same steady pace.

The cut continued to deepen and grow, exposing what seemed to be endless layers of threaded, grooved inner bark, now splintered and raw. Suddenly, the tree gave a dull groan as it leaned toward the side of the cut; reflex pulled the man backward out of range of the falling trunk and its many branches, which spread wide in a panicked tumble as the mass of nature crashed onto the woodland floor.

Wasting little time, the man set about cleaning the tree with his axe. He started from the cut, stepping back and forth across the bole as he worked his way up in a methodical sweep, removing any branches which were too green or too little to be of any use in the fire. But as he worked, he became aware of a small sound coming from somewhere nearby, toward the top of the fallen tree. He paid it no mind at first and kept working, yet the closer he got to the top, the louder the sound became; it now resembled a low, intermittent coo, an empty animal call carried on the sharp breeze. Unable to locate or identify this noise, the man looked around himself, searching the surrounding trees and overhead sky with curious eyes.

"Where in the world...?" he muttered to himself as the sound continued. Still without his answer, the man moved further up and around the fallen tree and there, at the very ends of its topmost branches, he found the source of the call.

On the forest floor sat a robin, fixed and unblinking. The only movement it made was to open its beak and let out that hollow cry;

its eyes never wavered and stared only straight ahead. Before it, about an arm's length away from where the bird sat, lay a jagged, upturned, brown nest with a single sky-blue egg, cracked and leaking. The fluid from the egg melted the fine frost that lingered on the ground, raising a delicate trail of steam up and through the sunlight.

The man stood watching, at first not daring to move. He waited several minutes and still the robin kept up its call, the feathers of its breast ruffling, rising, and falling with each strained note. For a moment the man's heart clenched, and he was suddenly struck by the feeling that this sound would follow him the rest of his life. The sound was loud enough for all the world. He continued to stand, rooted in place, as the seconds stretched on until all fell silent once more in the hollow of the woods; the egg had lost its warmth and the robin had gone, flown away on soundless wings. Slowly, the man came back to himself and realized the day was getting on. After removing the last trimmings, he cinched the rope around the log, knotted it with a few firm tugs and began the trek home.

It was near evening when he reached the cabin. His wife spotted him from the window and came outside to meet him. He hauled the tree along the final stretch into the yard, dropped the ends of the rope from his shoulders and, in a strained voice, asked about the child.

"Restless. I've used the last good pieces from the store making supper, so we'll need more wood for the night."

The man said nothing in reply, only picked up his axe and returned to work. He removed two weathered branches, enough to get them through to the morning, and went inside to eat, leaving the rest of the wood until tomorrow when it could be sawn, split and stacked. After the meal he crept over to the cot, but found the child still awake. He scooped it up, blankets and all, and moved closer to the hearth, from which there rose a procession of ragged grey clouds that disappeared up the chimney and through the cabin roof. The father held his bundle close and in a quiet, gentle voice began to hum a song he had first heard as a child.

Carol

DIANE KIRBY

I CARESS THE BLACK-AND-WHITE photograph, gently smoothing out the yellowed edges as I remember. The picture was taken on Christmas Day 1973 and shows a boy with long hair sitting between two girls on a cut velvet sofa. He is studying the scrapbook in his hands. The scrapbook was a gift intended to hold a collection of memories. And the trio, in their exuberance of youth, could not wait to fill it.

But as I look at this picture, I wonder what happened. The boy is dead. And a fair portion of me, the girl on the right, is gone, too. I am now a different woman trying to piece together the shattered remnants of my heart. And the girl on the left? She is the girl who introduced me and the boy to one another and witnessed our life together. She is, and has always been, my best friend.

When I was fourteen, my family moved to a new subdivision on the city limits. Instead of walking almost five kilometres to school, there was a school bus. And on day one of my school bus years, I met her. She was waiting for the bus too. The bus route went to several schools. She attended a different high school, but the rides were long enough for us to become fast friends. I lived in a quiet, stable home, whereas her home life was chaotic and toxic. She escaped to my house a lot. She liked my parents and they adored her. She became the sister I never had. In the years following my father's death, it was her and not me who made the journey to his grave in Scotland to raise a glass to him.

As teenagers, we talked long into the night about books, philosophy and art. We danced at a club called Purgatory in our latest fashion creations. We immersed ourselves in the music in coffee houses. We shared our limited knowledge and life experience while constantly seeking to expand our limits. She looked out for me and I for her. And we did it all while laughing. God, how we laughed!

She introduced me to the boy in the picture, a former boyfriend with whom she'd had a short-lived fling. She was my maid of honour when I married him. A typical Leo, she took credit for that. But she was as close to him as she was to me. A sister to both of us. And despite her relocation to British Columbia after college, we still saw her regularly. We went to visit her; she came to us. I also met up with her in several other countries over the years. She and I have dined in the Russian Tea Room in New York, gazed at art in The Hermitage in St. Petersburg, waited for the sun to rise at Angkor Wat and snorkelled off the coast of Cuba. And not one to be left out, the boy also had his moments with her. Together, they once rode across the entire length of the old Dundas Street bridge on the back wheel of his Harley. She still laughs as she tells it. And she smiles as she recalls the time they tasted rare whiskeys in Banff. None of us were surprised when he drove her to her home in the mountains from Ontario on his motorcycle. Her partner had just finished a year of touring South America, but their bike had broken down, so my husband stepped in to help.

The fact is that despite always living on the other side of the country, she was present at every significant event in our lives and many, many more minor ones. She fixed my hair the day I got married. She held me when a pregnancy ended. She showed me how to care for my new baby. She looked after my boys when they went out west to go skiing. She went to my son's wedding last summer with me. When I couldn't bring myself to give a speech, she stood up and eloquently welcomed the bride into our family for me. She has just always been there.

She is the one who met me in Amsterdam after the boy died suddenly and unexpectedly while riding his motorcycle. She sat quietly with me in a hotel room until past midnight waiting for my heart to stop breaking long enough for me to find my voice. I can't remember what she said. It seemed to me she was barely holding it together any better than I was. It sounded to me as if we were whispering. Or was it whimpering? Or was it both? We were both so wounded. I am not sure we ever—way back in those early days—envisioned that our relationship would include grieving together. Or, at the very least, her bearing witness to me trying desperately not to come apart at the seams.

She remains my anchor, the one who keeps me grounded and helps me make sense of our shared lives. She has become my last defence against becoming lost. She is the one person left who has known me the best and the longest. She is the one I hoped would remember me when I die. But I spoke to her today. And she is ill. She has had several bouts of melanoma and now the cancer is elsewhere. The prognosis is good... or so she says. Either way, I am shattered.

It seems that I have this misguided belief that I am getting by—until the next possible loss appears on the horizon and I realize that my entire hold on any of this life is tenuous at best. It is almost as wrong as the belief that we need a scrapbook to hold a collection of memories: I have volumes of scrapbooks filled with keepsakes and mementoes, but the lifetime of memories is in my heart.

The Rollercoaster

MARTHA MORRISON

My mother and I have driven hours and crossed the border for
    this moment:
Millennium Force, highest rollercoaster of the year 2000.
At the precipice, we anticipate the 89-degree drop,
hands clutched.

"Cancer is like a rollercoaster," the nurse says, decades later.
I protest. Rollercoasters are fun, cancer is not,
but we are already
plunging downwards,
barrelling toward the shimmering lake below. As I grasp at life,
    normalcy blurs past,
then out of sight.

My youngest baby is two months old
when the "C word" barges its way into our lexicon
and interrupts my postpartum bubble,
thrusting me down with no exhilaration.

Cancer, the unwanted visitor,
demanding our time and pulling my attention
(without bringing a casserole).

Cancer: the ride we can't get off,
looping my family around as we learn
about tumours, white blood cell count,
different types of chemotherapy.
Hurled around medical websites,
I stare at statistics while I breastfeed my infant,
hormones jerk me around like a banked turn into a spiral
before another big

drop.

Our toddler son doesn't understand
the long days away. Where is the sign
that says he is too small to ride?

CT scans, MRIs, breast pumps, waiting rooms, surgery, specialists.
The G-forces come multi-directionally.

Time slows and nerves twist before the results of the scans come in.
"Has it spread?" — the thought on every family member's mind,
uphill gravity weighing down each moment.
A headache throbs with the effort of holding back tears.
My toddler chatters like the clacks on the rails
as we live with constant worry.

Our baby says "Mama,"
glimmers of joy that weave through days.

My mother phones to discuss the news.
The treatment is working.
"We're not out of the woods yet,"
she cautions, for fear I would push off the heavy
safety harness
and jump off this ride altogether.
"But there's hope."
I exhale, mentally clutching her words to my heart,
the way I grasped her hands all those years before,
on the Millennium Force, hanging at the precipice.

Out of the Shadows on Chestnut Avenue

MACKENZIE HOWSON

Six years ago

S HE WALKED QUICKLY down the street. The late afternoon sun cast its golden light over the chestnut trees towering above the sidewalk.

She glanced at the community library box their neighbour Josh had built over the summer, a bright forest scene painted across the surface. *Shoot. I forgot those books again.*

Mr. Aziz at No. 114 was dragging his garbage and recycling bins to the curb for collection the following morning. She smiled and offered a quick hello. He nodded back with a wide grin. "Good evening."

She could feel the heat of the casserole dish she was carrying radiate through the oven mitts she was wearing. Her pace quickened and she heaved a sigh. She'd meant to drop this off for Gertrude an hour ago. The afternoon had slipped by and she was running behind. Her family's dinner was prepped, but in her rush to deliver Gertrude's casserole, she hadn't yet slid it into the oven.

Her husband would be home soon with their two-year-old son. It took them twice as long to get home now since they moved to the neighbourhood six months ago. But they knew it would be worth it.

She and her husband used to walk along the paths of the Thames River that led up to Chestnut Avenue, arms intertwined, dreaming of a child of their own to join the kids playing along the street, jokingly debating which house they would live in, and won over by the friendly openness of the people who lived here.

They hadn't yet found a suitable childcare provider closer to home, so weekdays were rushed in the evening, and they found themselves falling into bed exhausted only to wake early and do it all again. She kept reminding herself and her husband that life with a toddler was only a season. There was plenty to savour about this time, including their son's sweet chubby cheeks.

As she passed No. 111 her gaze landed on an older man in shabby clothes, rummaging through the garbage bin at the edge of the sidewalk. *He must've come up from the encampment.* They often did on the day before garbage day, hoping to find treasures cast off by the inhabitants of Chestnut Avenue.

Her friend Stacey, who lived at No. 111, had also taken to putting her bins out the night before, ever since Steve had left. She was now juggling everything on her own and Stacey's son was having a hard time. She wanted to do more to help. *I'll ask her for dinner this weekend.*

The man pulled something out of the bins, but before she could catch a glimpse her phone let loose a shrill ringing. She balanced the dish on her left hand, tucked the other oven mitt under her arm, and pulled the phone from her back pocket. Private caller. *He forgot to turn off work mode again.* She swiped her thumb across the screen to answer.

"Hey babe! I'm just dropping off—" She was interrupted by a grave voice she didn't recognize. She stood silently for a beat. The casserole dish slid from her hand. It hit the concrete. Ceramic and glass shattered as mashed potatoes, bits of green broccoli, stringy cheese and slices of honey-glazed ham splattered across the sidewalk. The crash reverberated throughout the neighbourhood.

Today

Tendrils of steam rise from the mug nested between her cupped hands. Gertrude sits at the kitchen table for two, the other chair vacant, and gazes into the backyard through the screen door across from her. Except for the changing seasons marking the passing of the past six years, the view remains unchanged.

She sighs and takes a sip of dark and bitter liquid, its heat fending off the sharp chill of the late-summer morning air. Sunshine just peeks over the trees that fall away to the river at the bottom of the steep slope at the back of her yard.

Her thoughts are interrupted by a clatter of glass and metal coming from the small garage at the side of her house.

"Damn raccoons," she grumbles.

She slams her mug down, tea sloshing over the lip, and pushes stiffly up against the surface of the table to get to her feet, grunting with the effort. *It's too early for this.* She goes to the screen door, grabbing the broom propped up in the corner. She steps out into the biting morning air and scowls. Her shawl is draped over the back of her chair. She makes her way down the steps, taking them one at a time, leaning on the rail for balance. As she rounds the corner of her house and looks through the doorway into the small garage, more a glorified shed, she sees a figure silhouetted in the darkness rummaging in the recycling bins.

"Hey!" she calls out sharply. "What are you doing?"

Tin cans clank and rattle, falling back into the recycling bin, and the figure joltingly shuffles toward her. Gertrude holds the broom in front of her to keep space between them. She volunteered at a soup kitchen downtown for years. She saw some of her regulars change dramatically, unpredictably, from overuse of drugs or alcohol or both. She's cautious. As the figure steps from the dark interior of the garage into the backyard, she sees a thin middle-aged woman. She squints a little, eyes adjusting to the growing sunlight, and is surprised to see the woman is actually much younger. *She must be in her thirties.* Grime from living in the woods is embedded into the lines in her face, her hands, darkening her nails. Her face is pale and, despite the cool morning air, beads of perspiration glisten across her forehead. Her body shakes. Her clothing is worn and stained, sagging loosely from her bony frame. A deep scratch cuts into the inner part of her left arm, angry redness radiating outwards. Her eyes are hollow and glassy, her breathing quick and laboured. She clutches a discoloured fabric tote bag to her side.

Gertrude sighs again, begrudgingly. "Do you need help?"

The younger woman is silent, staring.

Gertrude looks to the cut again, concern reflexively triggered by her many years as an ER nurse. "That's a nasty-looking cut. It really should be taken care of. Can I take a look at it?" She tries to remember what first-aid supplies she might still have on hand. She stopped maintaining her kit when her medical training wasn't enough to help Joe get better.

The other woman continues staring then pulls the handles of her bag apart, reaches in, pawing through the contents, and pulls something out. She hunches forward and lets it slip through her fingers. She turns to shuffle through the garage and out to the street before the older woman can catch up.

I should call someone. Gertrude remembers several community services she could call to help the younger woman in addition to the paramedics. *That'll have to do.*

Body stiff and weary, and using the broom for support, she moves forward to pick the dropped item up. She turns the cracked and chipped white clay heart over in her hand, a hole at the top where a ribbon once threaded through. On one side the words *Neighbours like you are precious and few!* are painted in a thin, curling script, and on the other *Steve and Stacey, thank you so much for the warm welcome!*

Steve and Stacey…across the street? I'll bring it by later.

But later comes and goes, and as Gertrude is drying the dishes after her early dinner she's interrupted by a knock at the door. She makes her way to the front door and slowly swings it open.

"Gertrude! Hi!" the woman at the door says, her smile not quite reaching her tired, sad eyes. "It's been so long. How are you doing?"

"Hello, Stacey. I'm doing fine, thanks. Yourself?"

"Oh…doing okay. Sorry to call on you out of the blue. I wanted to come by earlier but was running late for work. Was that Daphne I saw leaving your place this morning?"

"There was a woman from the encampment going through my bins first thing but I don't know her name. Is she a regular around here? Actually, she dropped something I think belongs to you. I was going to bring it over later. Just a sec." Gertrude goes to the kitchen to get the ornament from the counter where she'd left it, and brings it back, holding it out toward Stacey.

Stacey's face pales and she haltingly reaches for the ornament. "Daphne gave this to me. I threw this out years ago. After Steve left."

There's silence. Gertrude clears her throat, unsure of what to say. *How did I not know?* Changing the subject, she asks awkwardly, "I'm sorry, who is Daphne? How do you know her?"

Stacey looks up and says, "Oh…right…you might not have met them. Daphne, Rob and their son Luke moved into the neighbourhood around the time Joe got sick." Her voice falters. "There was a car accident…Rob and Luke didn't make it." She clears her throat, trying to keep from tearing up. "Everything fell apart for her after. She lives by the river now. So we see her from time to time, but she doesn't recognize us anymore. She's taken to bringing things she finds down by the river up to leave for the kids along the street. I wonder how she ended up with this," she murmurs, looking down at the ornament in her hands.

"Daphne…used to drop meals off for me, after…"

Stacey smiles sadly. "They very much jumped into being a part of the community. Daphne was a great friend…but she shut down, shut everyone out…"

Gertrude opens then closes her mouth. She once was part of this community, with Joe. "She has a cut on her arm that's infected pretty badly. I called city services, but I wish she would have let me take a look at it." She pauses. "I'd like to make sure she's okay— would you come down with me to find her? I'm not as steady on my feet these days."

Stacey offers an arm to Gertrude and they head out to the sidewalk.

Many of their neighbours are out enjoying the warmth of the late afternoon. Mr. and Mrs. Aziz stroll by hand in hand. Mrs. Aziz laughs at something Mr. Aziz says and playfully swats his arm. Two blonde girls go whizzing by on their bikes toward the park. *Were those the Teller twins? They must be sixteen or seventeen!* Josh Simpson and his wife Liv herd their three children along the opposite sidewalk, trying to keep the youngest two from stepping down onto the road or from wandering too far onto the neighbours' lawns. Gertrude remembers delivering a crocheted blanket she'd made for their eldest, but she's missed the birth of the younger two, now seemingly three and five. Liv notices Gertrude beside Stacey, smiles and calls out "Hello!" Gertrude nods her head in return.

They make their way up the street to the walking path that branches off from the sidewalk and meanders down through the wooded area beside the Thames. As they near the location of the encampment, blue tarp peeks through the trees. They step off the gravel path where the undergrowth has been trampled by the coming and going of those who live in the informal community that's taken root here. An older man sits by a fire contained within a rusted metal barrel roughly sawn in half. He is worn, face lined with wrinkles, ruddy from hard living and being in the elements for so long. His eyes are bleary, clothes stained a uniform brown. He grins widely, a mouth of missing and rotten teeth, weaving back and forth where he sits.

"You bringin' me anythin' today," he slurs.

"Not today, I'm afraid," Gertrude says gently.

"Pffft," he blows out, lifting a hand to wave dismissively at them.

"Actually, we're looking for someone," Gertrude continues. He keeps staring at the flames licking the inside walls of the barrel. "Her name is Daphne. Can you tell us which home is hers?"

Without looking up, the man says, "Daphne ain't here. She's gone."

"Can you tell me where she's gone to, or if you know when she'll be back?" Gertrude asks politely.

He looks over at the two women. "She got all tired and passed out after lunch. They said it was too late."

"Too late? What do you mean too late?" Gertrude presses.

"Them city people, they bring us stuff sometimes. Try to help," he spits. "They were here today with an ambulance. They couldn't wake her up. They said her blood was infected and that's that. She's not coming back."

Gertrude steps back and Stacey reaches out a hand to steady her. They look at each other sadly and make their way down the path to a spot that opens up on the riverbank. Roots of the over-hanging trees jut out, exposed from the rise and fall of the river, creating low benches for passersby to rest.

They sit watching the last rays of sunlight glitter on the ruffling surface of the flowing river. Crickets chirp. In the distance they hear the hoot of an owl.

"I'm so sorry," Gertrude says. "She was your friend."

"You did what you could," Stacey says.

"Hmmm…"

"Sometimes, there's just nothing we can do…no matter how much we want to," Stacey continues.

"I would like to have known her…I *could* have known her." Regret shadows Gertrude's words.

Stacey grasps Gertrude's hand. "We should get home," she whispers.

They don't speak until they're back on Chestnut Avenue.

"I'd like it if you could come for dinner one of these days. Maybe this weekend? Saturday?" Stacey says as they get to Gertrude's front door.

"I'd like that," Gertrude says with a quiet smile.

They say goodnight and Gertrude watches until the door at No. 111 latches shut. She enters her home and her eyes are drawn to a framed photo of her and Joe, surrounded by their children's families, hanging in the hall. Tears prickle in her eyes. But she smiles and runs a finger along the figure of her husband.

"Oh, how I miss you."

She goes to the kitchen, where the light glows warmly, and makes herself a cup of tea. She returns to her front porch where her little white wicker loveseat sits grey from years of disuse and exposure to the elements. *I'll clean it up tomorrow.* She sits with her hand resting where she and Joe once laced their fingers together. They would look out over the neighbourhood, talking about their children, reminiscing about their past, dreaming of their future. She gazes into the evening. The lamplights flicker on. She listens to the rustle of leaves in those steady, towering chestnut trees lining the street, still standing.

Firsts

DONNA COSTA

He was my first.

First boyfriend,
first kiss,
first slut-shamer.

We kissed in the graveyard behind the old stone church,
held hands in the lane.
He draped his leather jacket over my chilly shoulders.
He was sixteen; me, thirteen—an adolescent in a
well-developed body.

It was after I started seeing another boy,
one who bought me grape gumballs,
that he shouted it at me.

I was on the wooden swing when he passed by.
I didn't know what the word meant.
But I understood the loathing.
Years later, I heard he beat his wife.

First lucky escape.

Reunion

EMILY DE ANGELIS

At the edge of the gorge,
far from the shelter of the woods,
surface water seeps
downward,
gathering into rivulets
that creep through ancient escarpment crevices,
running a gauntlet of
cedar and jack pine roots
burrowed into limestone,
intertwined
defending
against haughty erosion.

Rain falls through leaf and needle
of horizonal trees—
branches growing outward from
the cliff's face
defying gravity—
and drip drops

running along vines and
trickling through
grooves in furrowed, dappled bark
forming canopy inkblots
where they fall
on flat, dusty stone below.

At the bottom of the ravine,
rushes and sedges take root,
lush grasses along the marsh edge,
marginal fortification
against flood waters and runoff,
filtering forward
into fern and duckweed
flowing through watershed kidneys.
Silt and sediment trapped.
Held back by nature's fortitude,
while pristine water gurgles
into creek and stream,
tributaries that crisscross
the valley floor,
between mountains,
to a reunion with the river.

A Trinity of Trials

J. EDWARD ORCHARD

I STOWED MY BACKPACK—EMBLAZONED with a red maple leaf—in the overhead compartment, squeezed my lanky frame into the window seat, and did my best to stop shaking.

It was my first time travelling abroad, and my first time on an airplane. I pulled some folded papers from my back pocket, and shifted in my seat to get comfortable. The papers detailed the story of two men, Terrence Tully and James Medcalf, who attempted to fly from London, Ontario to London, England in September of 1927. Carling Brewery held a contest at the time with a prize of $25,000 for the first to accomplish the feat.

I was interested in Tully and Medcalf's story, and I liked the symmetry of flying from one London to the other London. Thinking it an adventure, I signed up for a government-sponsored work-abroad program. But now, on a hazy August morning in 1990, minutes before the flight was to take off, the magnitude of the undertaking began to weigh on me.

An elderly South Asian man in an immaculate white cotton kurta sat down beside me. He bowed his head politely as I unfolded the papers.

"You're a good boy," he said in a paternal manner, patting my arm. I wasn't so certain about that, but gave a sheepish nod. I had a tidy Oxford haircut at the time, neatly parted and tapered at the back and sides. Newly out of college, I fancied myself a man of the world. Really, I was just a naive, pasty-faced kid from the suburbs of WASP Canada with more blemishes than brains. I had never been outside my province, let alone my country. What did I know? I was scared out of my mind.

The Air Ontario CV580 turboprop aircraft clattered and shook like a roller coaster car at the Western Fair. I bounced in my seat, white-knuckled the armrests and felt my stomach lurch. Ears popping, heart racing, I wondered if Tully and Medcalf's takeoff sixty-three years earlier in their fabric-covered, wood strut monoplane had been any smoother than this.

The intense shaking lasted only a few minutes, but it felt like a lifetime to me. My seatmate in the kurta, on the other hand, sat Zen-like, smoothing out the wrinkles on his sleeves. He smiled at me, and patted my forearm again.

His reaction to such things, I thought, was a sign of his maturity and worldliness. I began to breathe easier, and found it helpful to look out the window at the receding blanket of green that gave the Forest City its name.

Little was I aware that in the months to come, I would travel my own ragged path to maturity, recalling formative experiences along the way and making deals with myself as coping mechanisms. Three incidents in particular were defining moments.

A couple of weeks after arriving in the UK, I found a job through the office of the British Universities North America Club. I was hired by a company called Sigma Security. Tensions were high in the Middle East leading up to the first Gulf War. The BBC hired Sigma to protect its staff. I was stationed at Bush House, in central London, the headquarters of the BBC World Service.

Two guards were to be at the front entrance at all times, on rotating twelve-hour shifts, checking the IDs of everyone who passed through the building's ornate wrought iron gates. On my second shift, clad in a thick cotton uniform reminiscent of that worn by World War I soldiers, I worked with George, an army veteran, and Addison, a bearded stoic stationed at the front desk of the building.

George was short, taciturn and tightly coiled, in the way a cornered wolverine might be. About five hours into the shift, pacing back and forth on the polished marble floors like a caged animal, he spoke.

"Where are you from?"

"Canada," I replied. "Where are you from?"

"Ireland."

"Ah," I said. I knew of Ireland being divided from Northern Ireland, so, thinking myself clever, asked: "Which Ireland are you from?"

Addison winced.

"I'll tell ya, son," George barked, fixing me with cobalt steel-coloured blue eyes that could melt iron. "There's only one Ireland!"

The separation of north from south was a source of great conflict in Ireland. I realized the insensitivity of my question too late.

A tense silence ensued. The second hand on the teak grandfather clock in the lobby of Bush House ticked slowly. At one point, the director of the World Service entered. He was a pear-shaped man with a year-round suntan. Clearly accustomed to waves parting before him wherever he walked, he moved with purpose in an impeccable charcoal-coloured Armani suit and red silk tie. He spoke his name aloud as he attempted to pass George.

George stepped in front of him, and asked for his identification. The director repeated his name tersely. George stood firm.

"I don't care what your name is, boyo. Everyone shows ID."

"Good evening, Director," Addison said, without raising his voice. "Good to see you. I'll take it from here, thank you, George."

Addison rose from his seat to escort the director down the hallway to his office.

When the shift ended, in the locker room where we changed out of our uniforms, George walked toward me. My right fist clenched involuntarily. I imagined myself writing a letter to my mother from an English hospital bed: *Dear Mom, I've been beaten to a pulp by a mad Irish Army veteran with a grudge against the world. Tell my brother Greg he can have my comic books. Love, Jeff.*

George extended his right hand quick as an alley cat. I jumped back, practically falling over one of the locker room benches.

"Ya seem like a good man," he said, catching my right hand to shake it as I stumbled. "But you can't trust anyone, especially if you're a Paddy like me in London, what with the Troubles and all. They don't respect a Dub here. And, I'll tell ya," he said, broad smile crossing his face and belying his earlier countenance completely, "there's only one Ireland!"

In time, I learned that to George, Bush House was English imperialism personified.

"I sense it with every step on the polished stone floors," he said, "smell it in the finish of the wood panelling, and feel it to me core with every high and mighty look from the public-school prats who run the place."

Heading home after a night of drinking with some work colleagues in the autumn of 1990, I gingerly made the climb to street level at the train station in Stoke Newington, in Northeast London. I opened the door to the station lobby. I was greeted by an enormous bald man dry-shaving his head with a rusted razor.

"What you doing here, you fucking cunt?!" he bellowed.

I shook my head in a vain effort to clear my senses and shoo away the dark apparition. "I'm sorry, do I know you?"

The man's head was scarred with dried blood. He wore black high-top Doc Martens boots, ripped denim pants and a tattered, oil-stained sweatshirt. He had to be three hundred pounds and looked like a nightmare vision of a Neo-Nazi skinhead.

"What a load of bollocks!"

I looked frantically around the grimy glass-walled vestibule that was the station exit. There was no one else in sight, and the lacerated leviathan was blocking the turnstiles to the street outside.

The man took a step toward me, waving the disposable razor over his head like a miniature lasso. I backed into the stairwell door, right hand clutching for the handle.

"What you doing here, I says!"

Then, in a moment of recognition, my mind flashed to a darkened movie theatre two years earlier. I was watching *The Shining* with my friend when a man stood up at the far end of our row. The man frantically crossed in front of people, striking knees and elbows. People cursed and yelled at him to sit down. My friend, on the other hand, stood up and offered the man his hand. "This way," he said. "I can help you. The aisle is just over here." The man took his hand and my friend helped him to the theatre lobby. My friend had recognized that the man had a disability and was in crisis.

I sensed something similar about the man in front of me.

I stepped to the right, looking to see if the man's eyes would follow mine. They didn't. He continued to stare straight ahead. He wasn't looking at me; he was looking *through* me. He wasn't seeing me at all as he strode forward cursing, raging at some phantom from long ago only he could see.

"What you doing here! That what I says to him." He reached the stairwell exit where I had been, and began pounding on the door, razor still clutched in his right fist. "Stay away from Lizzy! You'll never have her for yourself! No bloody way!"

He turned and collapsed to the floor, sobbing, right hand falling open, streaked with blood, razor coming to rest near the edge of his palm.

"No bloody way. No bloody way…"

"It's all right," I said, pulling some pub napkins from my pocket and kneeling down. "He's not here anymore." Reaching out, I placed two of the napkins in the palm of his hand, folded the remaining one gently over the razor and slowly picked it up.

Rising to my feet, I backed away from the fallen giant. He pulled his knees up to his chest and began to rock back and forth.

I treaded on the discarded page of a broadsheet newspaper as I pushed my way through the turnstiles into the night air. The newspaper headline read *Cuts to National Mental Health Service Hurt Those Who Need It Most.*

Feeling suddenly very sober, I found a nearby police box, wishing to alert someone before the man could hurt himself any further.

Several months later, I was travelling from London to the west coast of Wales by bicycle. I made one side trip in between youth hostels to visit my friend's relatives in the Rhymney Valley. The family were warm and welcoming, treating me to a late afternoon meal of newspaper-wrapped fish and chips. I stayed later than intended, but figured I had plenty of time to get to the next youth hostel, twenty-seven miles' travel, before dark.

I was wrong.

The air was thick and damp as I cycled north out of the village. My second-hand ten-speed creaked and complained. The going was slow on the narrow backroads. Dusk fell by the time I turned onto an old dirt laneway into Brecon Beacons National Park.

My bike lamp offering only a faint glow, I relied on moonlight and the sound of the gravel beneath my tires to navigate. A thick stand of black alders flanked the road like eerie sentinels.

In the distance, I could hear a whisper on the night wind. Or was it a howl? Faint at first, then steadily clearer, the sound was plaintive and strained. I thought I must be hearing the fearsome Hound of the Baskervilles.

I was reminded of a time two years prior on the trails of Meadowlily Woods back home. My dog, a large Labrador retriever, growled and barked, and scared off a coyote who had happened onto the path in front of us.

I didn't have the benefit of a seventy-five-pound dog now. There were no police boxes nearby. It was just me on a rickety bicycle well past its best-before date. I began making deals with myself again, saying prayers to some newly enshrined Welsh deity.

The timbre of the pained baying ebbed and flowed, doing somersaults in my imagination. This monster was Grendel, fell minion of darkness. No, it must be the mythical Red Dragon, a creature so feared it adorns the very flag of Wales itself as a dread reminder.

I asked myself, what would my friend in the immaculate white kurta do to get out of these accursed woods? What would Tully and Medcalf have done?

In very Canadian fashion, I apologized. To my mother, for all I'd done wrong, and to my sister, for reading her diary when I was twelve.

"There's nothing in the darkness that isn't there in the light," my mother once said as we sat around a fire at a campground in Oriole Park, Komoka. "Maybe," my father joked, looking off into the darkened forest, "but you can't see it!"

THWUMP!!

I had the sensation of floating as in a dream. Water droplets hung in the air like sparkling crystals in the moonlight. I perceived my bicycle helmet spinning into the night mist beside me. I landed on a bed of fleece.

The bed moved and gave an annoyed bleat. Bodies of thick sodden wool shifted. Hooves scraped the gravel. I tumbled onto the ground.

Here was my Hound of the Baskervilles, here my Grendel. These were my frightful Red Dragons: a flock of grumpy, groaning Welsh mountain sheep gathered in the middle of the country lane. I'd ridden straight into them.

I pushed a couple of protesting woolly-backs aside as I struggled to stand. Massaging the back of my neck, I looked at the warped front tire of the bicycle. I had to smile. Sometimes it isn't the wolves you need to watch out for, but the sheep.

I donned the mantle of good shepherd and scattered the flock, leading them off the road with apples and carrots I had packed in my bike bags.

Soaked to the skin and smelling like a wet sweater, I finally arrived at the youth hostel at midnight.

"Ah, you would be Jeff," the innkeeper said. "Glad you could make it. I see you encountered Farmer Davies' flock. They've been the bane of many unsuspecting travellers."

Hair long, wearing faded jeans and clutching a dog-eared copy of Kerouac's *On the Road*, I made my way to my seat on the 737 bound for Canada. It was a year to the day since I'd begun my travels. I thought about Tully and Medcalf, the daring young men in their fragile flying machine. They never made it home, but they blazed the trail for transatlantic flights, for people like me to leave the relative shelter of the Forest City, to step out into the world at large, to face their fears, real and imagined, and maybe return home a little wiser for it.

A young child in the seat next to mine looked at me imploringly. As the jet thundered into the air from Gatwick airport, she held tightly to her mother's hand, and reached for mine. I glanced over at her mother, who nodded. Thinking of my own maiden flight on that shaky CV580, I smiled, patted the girl's forearm, took her hand, and offered what comfort I could.

Schrödinger's Hamster

JAN SIMS

ZACH DIDN'T KNOW what was more annoying—the shrieks from the neighbourhood kids playing road hockey, or the creaky hamster wheel in his brother's room.

Any annoyance becomes a much bigger deal when you're stuck in your bedroom, he figured.

The creaky hamster wheel was a no-brainer. Anyone would be bothered by that. The road hockey was a bit more complicated.

Zach didn't believe in emotional intelligence. But that's exactly what Andy from across the street possessed and Zach sorely lacked. Andy could always get a bunch of kids to come together and have fun. No one was left behind, even Zach's little brother Danny, who didn't know one end of a hockey stick from the other.

Enough staring out the window at the stupid hockey game, back to ancient Rome. Zach booted up his computer.

"Parents can be so stupid," Zach muttered to himself. "They think sending me to my room is a punishment? I'd be here anyway." Zach had been researching Roman military campaigns. He was already up to the emperor Trajan.

Zach was hardly going to take the time to think about the

reason for being sent to his room. He wasn't sorry in the slightest. For the record, it had to do with the day camp that his parents signed him up for. *Phun with Physics!* was the title, which Zach considered absolutely ridiculous. He'd tried to talk his parents out of sending him there, arguing, among other things, that he was intellectually way beyond the things that would be taught to the other eleven-year-olds. But his parents dug in, saying they'd already paid the deposit.

Payback came in the form of a Facebook group the camp had set up for the kids. "Facebook? Seriously? Why don't they just have us communicate with sheets of papyrus," Zach had groaned. But that didn't stop him from posting a sarcastic response to the question asked by the camp counsellors, "What do you expect to learn from *Phun with Physics?*" Zach's reply: "Sweet Ph*ck All!"

Zach lost track of time as he immersed himself in Trajan's campaign against the Parthians, Rome's enemy to the east. He didn't hear Danny come into his room, or the scratching sounds from the shoebox his brother held.

"I'm probably not supposed to be in here. I know you're being punished and stuff," Danny whispered. "I thought you might like some company." Danny reached out with the shoebox and a hopeful smile. "You can play with Socks."

Socks.

It was a truly stupid name for a hamster, Zach had pointed out when they arrived home from the store after his parents made good on a promise to get the boys a pet. His mom had vetoed the idea of a rat—which was Zach's first choice because of its intelligence—making reference to some rat-related movie she'd seen as a child that totally freaked her out.

A hamster it was. And Danny was resolute in calling it Socks.

Zach explained that while it might be an okay name for a cat or dog because of their markings, it made no sense to call a hamster

Socks because, well, their feet or legs or whatever were just a non-descript shade of red.

Danny had turned seven in the months since the pet store outing, and he still thought Socks was a cool name for a hamster.

"Schrödinger's cat," Zach mumbled as he took the shoebox from Danny, not caring that he might be violating the terms of his punishment by talking to his brother.

"What?" Danny tried to give the hamster a reassuring pat.

"Your hamster reminds me of a scientific theory, seeing him in the box like that."

Zach figured he'd better simplify the explanation, and he gestured for Danny to sit on the bed.

"It's a concept that was made famous by a physicist named Schrödinger," Zach began. "It postulates, um, *says* that if you put a cat in a box along with something that could kill it, you wouldn't know whether the cat was dead or alive until you opened the box."

Danny looked worried. "Poor kitty, that's really mean…"

"Let me explain," Zach interrupted. But Danny was having none of it.

"Did they at least give the kitty something to eat or drink?"

"Just let me finish." Zach was getting frustrated.

"Well, you have to make sure they get lots of water. Animals like to drink a lot of water," Danny said, gesturing to Socks.

"Shut up and listen to me!" Zach took a deep breath. "Never mind."

"No, I want to know," Danny implored.

Know what? Zach wanted to ask. *Quantum mechanics?* Instead, he just tousled his brother's hair. It was impossible for anyone, even Zach, to get mad at Danny. His little brother was just too genuinely nice.

"Let's talk about it another time, okay?"

Later that day, his punishment over, Zach joined his family for a backyard barbecue. He had to admit that despite their shortcomings, his parents knew how to grill a steak. Zach dug in, as his father talked about the pickup truck he was working on as a hobby. It was one of many interests they didn't share.

One day, Zach vowed, he'd write a book for parents and call it *How to Raise a Gifted Child: the Facts.*

Fact: It's a mistake to think gifted kids get excluded from neighbourhood stuff when they're little. Zach couldn't begin to count the number of playdates he'd been invited to over the years. "*Sorry,*" he'd wanted to tell the hopeful parents. "*Playing with me won't make your son or daughter suddenly interested in learning the periodic table of elements. Being gifted isn't something you can re-gift.*"

"Compulsory socialization," as Zach called it, came to an end when he outright told his parents that he would not take part in organized sports beyond peewee soccer. They'd sighed in disappointment but didn't force the issue.

These days, Zach just hung out with other kids from his special education class.

Fact: Gifted children usually have parents who excel in their professions. Zach's friend Trinity's mom was a renowned orthopaedic surgeon. Salinger's dad produced award-winning podcasts about social justice warriors. Zach's dad was a warehouse worker, and his mom hosted in-home parties selling Naughty 'n Nice lingerie. In his case, Zach didn't think the apple just fell far from the tree; it was from an entirely different orchard.

Over the years, his parents had encouraged him to "keep it real," as they would say. And truth be told, Zach genuinely enjoyed many of the enrichment-free activities that were part of his upbringing, especially the waterslides. He just kept that quiet among his super-smart friends.

Zach also didn't tell them about his family's relaxed nutritional standards.

He was finishing a bowl of Choco Loco Puffblasters for

breakfast one morning when Danny rushed into the kitchen. He practically tore the coffee cup from his mother's hand.

"Come quick," Danny pleaded.

Zach and his dad looked up in surprise. Nothing ever seemed to faze Danny.

"I think there's something wrong with Socks." Danny tugged his mom's housecoat as she tried unsuccessfully to put her coffee cup back on the table without spilling anything.

Danny ran ahead to his bedroom as his parents and Zach followed.

"I think we need to take Socks to the vet," Danny said as he opened the cage.

Socks was lying on his back.

Everyone, except Danny, knew that a vet wouldn't do any good.

"I'm sorry sweetie, but I think Socks has gone to hamster heaven," Zach's mom gently explained as Danny lifted Socks from the cage and began to nuzzle him.

Danny was inconsolable. That night he slept with his mom and dad in their big bed, while Zach and Socks both spent the night staring at the ceiling. Of course, in Socks' case it wasn't because of insomnia.

The next morning, Zach overheard his parents in their bedroom talking about what should be done with the dead hamster.

"We can't just leave it there in the cage," his father said. "It probably already has *rigor mortis*."

Zach was about to jump into the conversation and offer his medical research skills, but for once he just shut up.

"I know, I know," his mother sighed. "How about this," she continued after a moment's thought. "We take Socks out to the woods behind the house, and have kind of a hamster funeral?"

"Do you think Danny will be okay with that?" His father sat down on the bed.

"I don't know, but I can't think of any better ideas," his mother shrugged.

And so it was determined that a family funeral would take place for Socks.

Danny asked if he should wear black, but his parents said it wasn't necessary. He helped his mother find an appropriate coffin for Socks, which turned out to be a small, empty box meant for a set of Naughty 'n Nice panties.

There may be no such thing as a nice day for a funeral, and Socks' farewell certainly lived up to that. As a light rain fell, the little family trudged up the hill to the woods that backed onto their property. Danny held on tightly to the panties box.

Zach helped his dad dig a small hole in the earth, while his mother stroked Danny's hair. "I think we should all say something about Socks before we lay him to rest," Zach's mother announced. "I remember how proud we were of Danny, and how well Danny looked after him," she continued. "Zach, tell us your thoughts about Socks."

"Um…Socks was a…hamster… with brown and white markings," Zach stammered.

"Surely there's something else you could say," his mother hissed.

Zach knew that his parents wanted him to say something profound to help ease his brother's pain. But he was simply unwilling to go against one of his core beliefs—that once something or someone is dead, that's it. As for the concept of celebrating a life, Zach thought that was patently ridiculous for a hamster.

As Danny wiped his tears, his father gently took the box away from his son and put it in the hole that had been dug.

Danny's mother had prepared lasagna for dinner that night. It was Danny's favourite. But no one said much or asked for seconds.

The next morning only brought more of the depressing drizzle that had been falling at the funeral. Zach woke to the smell of waffles—another of Danny's favourites.

"Danny, Zach…breakfast is ready," his mother called, trying to inject a note of cheerfulness into her voice.

Zach stumbled downstairs and reached into the kitchen fridge to get the orange juice.

"Where's Danny?" His mother carefully lifted the waffles from the grill.

"Don't know. Maybe he's still sleeping." Zach took a gulp of juice.

"Do you mind going upstairs to see what's keeping him? He's usually the first one of us awake."

Zach went upstairs and opened the door to his brother's room. Danny wasn't there.

"Sorry Mom, he's not in his room," Zach said as he returned to the kitchen and popped a piece of waffle in his mouth.

"Where on Earth could he be at this hour?" His mother sounded more curious than alarmed.

"Dunno. You want me to check out back?"

"Sure, if you don't mind." A note of concern was creeping into her voice.

Zach looked all around the yard, while his mom and dad searched the house.

No Danny.

"This isn't like him," his mother said, shaking her head and covering the waffles with tinfoil.

It was at that moment Zach turned and saw the pile of empty boxes on the dining room table that his mom was getting ready for a Naughty 'n Nice home party.

"Schrödinger's cat," Zach muttered.

His parents looked puzzled.

"It's the famous concept. You know, the one with the cat and the box. I think I may know where Danny's gone. Just follow me outside."

With Zach leading the way, they made their way to the woods behind their house.

That's where they found Danny. He'd dug up the grave.

"I—I—thought Socks might still be alive," he sobbed.

"Oh, Danny, whatever gave you that idea?" His mother reached into her housecoat pocket for a tissue.

"It's like what Zach told me about the kitty cat. The one in the box that no one knew was dead or alive."

"I'll tell you all about it later," Zach assured his parents.

"You're really smart." Danny wiped his nose and looked up at Zach. "Is Socks really dead?"

Zach felt something stir within himself. Call it a conscience.

"Yes, Danny, he is. But you know what?" Zach sat down on the ground beside his little brother. "Maybe there really is a hamster heaven. And Socks is there."

"Huh?" his father exclaimed.

Zach's moral compass hadn't exactly been finely tuned over the years. Sure, his parents had taught him right from wrong. But when Zach was little and pestered them for the rationale behind concepts like empathy, they just shrugged and said something like: "It's the right thing to do."

The family wasn't big into organized religion, and that suited Zach just fine. He knew his parents were good people. If they couldn't explain abstract ideas like grief to Zach's satisfaction, no biggie.

What came next was totally out of character for Zach.

"Hamster heaven is the most beautiful place there ever was. With lots and lots of really good wheels for them to run around on." Zach put his arm around his brother.

"Do they get good stuff to eat?" Danny asked hopefully.

"Only the best," Zach smiled. "Fresh lettuce, not that fifty-percent-off stuff that Mom gets at the supermarket because it's a bargain."

"Hey, wait a second."

Zach ignored his mother. He was busy formulating in his

mind a picture of hamster heaven that rivalled the Elysian Fields. At the centre of it was Socks, in all his brown-and-white-furred, red-pawed glory.

It felt good to give Danny hope, even if Zach actually still believed that Socks' eternity was confined to a cardboard box designed for women's underwear.

After Zach had finished his epic description of hamster heaven, Danny blew his nose and handed the box containing Socks to his big brother.

"Will I ever see Socks again?" he asked quietly.

"I'm not sure," Zach answered truthfully. "But maybe…"

Zach put the box in the ground and packed it over with dirt.

For the second time in as many days, the family said goodbye to Socks.

Only this time, it was a proper hamster funeral.

COVID-19

MARI JOHNSON

O N MARCH 11, 2020, the weather was cold and overcast in London, Ontario. Dorothy turned on the news and heard that COVID-19 had been declared a pandemic. Hundreds had died and the grim news terrified her. These days even a mild cold left her struggling to breathe.

She pulled on a black beret, tucked in wisps of white hair, slipped on a beige parka and drove to the medical centre. "I need to see Dr. Smith. It's urgent," she said to the receptionist.

"You don't have an appointment, Mrs. O'Brien."

The family physician came to the front desk. "What's the problem, Mrs. O'Brien?"

"It's the pandemic, Dr. Smith. Patrick passed away six months ago and I have no one to care for me if I catch COVID."

"Wear a mask, isolate, and use your puffer," he replied without missing a beat and headed for his consultation room.

His indifference crushed Dorothy, and she drove to Walmart feeling depressed.

Masks were sold out so she went to Shoppers, paid extra for a box, and sat in the parking lot paralyzed with uncertainty. *What if truckers die bringing food from California to Ontario? And supposing humanity ceases to exist and I'm the last woman left wandering through deserted supermarkets like in a science fiction movie?* The thoughts galvanized her. She turned the key in the ignition, drove to Bulk Barn, and bought three large sacks of rice and three bags of dried beans.

When she returned to her red-brick, ranch-style home, Dorothy slowly carried the dried goods downstairs, one heavy load at a time, and stored them on basement shelves.

Upstairs, she glanced at the photo of her deceased husband and said, "Glad that's done, Pat. At least we won't starve."

Dorothy picked up her rosary, grasped the gold Celtic cross and green prayer beads, and recited the Our Father and Hail Mary.

"It's a form of meditation, Pat," she explained to her husband's photo, then wondered why she was still making excuses to the image of a lapsed Catholic, and rolled her eyes.

After lunch, she felt more relaxed and phoned her friend. "Hi Jan, want to go for a walk? We can wear masks and take Donnie. How is that cheeky mutt?"

"Donnie's fine, Dot, but I'm not up to it."

"Maybe later in the week, then. Talk soon!"

Dorothy hung up, placed essentials in a fanny pack, put on her parka and hat, and drove to the Thames River trail. The sound of rippling water and the spring sunshine lifted her spirits. Vines were gaining a foothold, with last year's withered vegetation serving as a frame for new tendrils. *They'll outlive both the virus and humanity*, Dorothy thought morosely, her mind slipping back to the pandemic.

A sudden noise like a cavalry charge surprised her as a large, white-tailed buck and doe galloped past, leaving a cloud of grey plant litter floating in their wake. Dorothy stood transfixed; it was a magical moment, a nature film brought to life.

A few minutes later, a dark outline up ahead on the trail turned out to be a large snapping turtle. Lifting the motionless creature by its shell, she dropped the heavy reptile by the riverbank. She suspected animals were losing their fear because people were isolating.

When the evening news reported COVID-19 was spreading in China and Italy, Dorothy cut an unbleached coffee filter to provide an extra liner for her mask. But the filter restricted her breathing and she had to remove it.

At 11 p.m. she set her alarm for 6:30 a.m., determined to be first in line at the supermarket.

Dorothy arrived by 7:15 a.m. and several shoppers were already there. As she looped the new, paper mask over her ears, her glasses fogged over. *Masks* can't *be 100% effective. Better avoid the store at peak hours and skip the trail on weekends*, she warned herself, and tried not to breathe deeply in hopes of reducing any viral load.

✍

Just before Christmas, the news announced a COVID vaccine was available. "Hey Pat, best Christmas present ever," Dorothy said, longing for an answer. But the faint sibilance of the clock marking every second was like a beating heart to remind her that time could be running out.

A sudden clatter broke the silence and she rushed to the bedroom window. The neighbour children were banging pots and pans to support healthcare workers. She found the clamour strangely comforting. Her peace of mind, however, didn't last.

Sitting alone on New Year's Day, she worried the vaccine was being distributed too quickly and phoned her friend. "Hey, Jan. I'm scared. What if the virus kills us?"

"You're alone too much, Dot. Get a dog!" Janet said.

As if a pet's a pill that can cure anxiety, Dorothy thought sarcastically as she hung up.

"If I get a puppy, what if dog food runs out?" she asked Patrick that evening. "Not that you'd care, riding on your white horse," she said, staring at the image of her smiling husband at Circle R Ranch.

When a light dusting of snow appeared that week, Dorothy cleared the patio and threw down birdseed. Doves and grey juncos landed after she shut the door, clawing over scattered grain that resembled sprinkles across a frosted cake. A squirrel scrabbled onto the top step, and she opened the door a crack, crouched down and held out a peanut. "Here ya go, Blacky," she said, blocking him with her foot as he tried to enter the house. He grabbed the peanut, checked for imperfections, stuffed the nut into his cheek and hurried away.

A chipmunk appeared next. "Hello, Chippy!" The creature squinted myopically on its hind legs, a white bib and snaggletooth adding more pathos to its persona as a seasoned panhandler. She tipped a shot glass full of birdseed onto the step, and the chipmunk hoovered the seeds into each pouch and disappeared in a flash. When she went back inside and shut the door, the juncos returned. "I have such a busy life," Dorothy announced to the empty room.

❧

Dorothy's garden bloomed with mimosa and forsythia, signalling an early spring. She woke up from a nap in her recliner by an open window with a tight chest and sore throat. She couldn't catch her breath. *Call an ambulance*, a voice echoed in her head. *But the hospital's full of COVID patients, and what if I don't have the virus?* she reasoned. A sensation of pins and needles began in her fingertips; she was breathing in short, shallow bursts and felt dizzy. "You're okay, you're okay. It's a panic attack," she whispered, reaching for her rosary and stroking the smooth beads that felt like Patrick's hand.

That night, she held the rosary wrapped in her fist, and in the morning, her breathing had improved. In the bathroom, Dorothy glanced at her reflection in the vanity mirror. "Lucky you. It's only seasonal allergies," she said.

After making oatmeal, she sat at the table with Patrick's photo. "I won't be joining you just yet, after all, Pat." She grimaced at his disingenuous smile.

In March, the Middlesex-London Health Unit announced that people over eighty could get the vaccine. The clinical trials had been of short duration, but unlike thousands who were afraid to be "guinea pigs," Dorothy was more fearful of the virus.

"Okay, okay, I'll get it," she told Patrick, as she sensed he urged her not to waste time. After trying to book online for hours, she finally got through.

Two days after her shot, her arm stopped aching and she headed for the trail. As she rounded the bend past the bridge, a woman with hiking poles stood motionless, staring across the meadow.

"Look over there," the woman said excitedly, her voice muffled behind a bulky red scarf. She pointed to a herd of grazing deer.

Dorothy counted fifteen adults and a few young ones. *Here it is, a snapshot of tomorrow,* she thought. *Animals have taken over, and this stranger and I are like a couple of survivors, scrounging for our existence.* Dorothy had allowed her imagination to run wild and knew it was a mistake. The nature trail had turned into a nightmare of possibilities, and she returned home feeling depressed.

The next morning at 7 a.m., she grabbed her purse and car keys, and left for the supermarket. Inside the store, she used the hand sanitizer on the wall and deftly pinched the wire across her mask. Ahead of her, a woman wearing a plastic face shield and latex gloves paused in the throes of a dry cough. Dorothy changed direction and held her breath until it was safe to breathe.

She placed her selection of canned soups and frozen entrées on the belt at the checkout. The cashier used to chat but now stood behind her plexiglass shield and stared. They had become strangers, and Dorothy felt their silence was a shared moment of remembrance for those who had died from the virus.

At home, she unpacked her groceries and slumped into her

chair. The four walls once evoked happy memories, but the images were locked away. This house was now her prison and she was being detained against her will by a viral enemy. She dropped her head in her hands and wept.

⁓

The weeks were interminable. To kill time, Dorothy bought *The London Free Press* to read the obituaries and complete the crossword puzzle.

One morning in May, she was filling in the blanks and remembered Patrick had called the puzzle "juvenile."

"Where's your fancy *Globe and Mail* cryptic crossword now, smarty-pants?" she asked Patrick's photo. The ghost on his white horse appeared to be smirking at her.

Janet phoned that evening. "How are you doing, Dot? Anything new?"

"Same old," Dorothy replied. "Let's get together soon, Jan. I can't stand the isolation. I feel like I'm going nuts. We can sit outside pretty soon."

Warm weather arrived and Dorothy met Janet outside her house. They wore masks and sat on lawn chairs three metres apart to avoid viral droplets. Janet's grey hair hung loose around her shoulders, and Dorothy thought she looked like a neglected dementia patient.

"Hairdressers must be going out of business, Jan. D'ya want me to give you a trim?"

Janet glanced at Dorothy's white hair and grinned. "No thanks, Dot. I'm good."

She probably thinks I hacked it with blunt garden shears, Dorothy thought.

"Who's a good boy, then, eh, Donnie?" Dorothy gently massaged the Jack Russell's muzzle as he stared up at her.

"Must be hard to lose Patrick after sixty years, Dot. I know what that feels like."

"Pat could be difficult, Jan, but I still talk to him. Stops me from going crazy. Let's go for a short walk and take the dog." Dorothy stood up and groaned, massaging her lower back as Donnie trembled with anticipation, leaped in the air and spun round in circles.

❧

The trees were bare in late fall when Omicron appeared as a variant of COVID-19, more contagious but less severe than the original strain. "I think the virus is losing its death grip," Dorothy said to Patrick.

But the isolation was taking its toll. When the news still reported catastrophic numbers of COVID victims, Dorothy grieved for these strangers. She prayed that she and Janet would continue to stay safe, and turned to a black-and-white world of sixties movies while waiting for conditions to improve.

In the spring, as trees released their pollen, Dorothy used a new rapid test to rule out COVID, and a single pink line indicated she was negative. Sighing with relief, she used her asthma inhaler and was glad no one she knew had caught the virus.

After visiting Janet, the weather turned cool and wet, and she did not hear from her friend for two weeks. When the skies cleared, she knocked on Janet's door and her daughter, Maggie, opened it.

"Dorothy, I'm so sorry I haven't called sooner. It's Mom. She passed away two days ago from COVID."

Dorothy gasped and grabbed the door frame to steady herself. "That's terrible news, Maggie, I'm so sorry."

"Mom wasn't bad at first. The hospital gave her Paxlovid, but she got worse and ended up on a ventilator. Mom had a good life. She was eighty-six, and you were a good friend. We'll hold a memorial service for her later."

"I'm so sorry," Dorothy repeated as Donnie peered anxiously up at her from between Maggie's legs.

Dorothy returned home and picked up her husband's photo. "Janet was my best friend, Patrick. I'll miss her and Donnie so much," she cried.

‿

Shortly after Easter 2023, masks became optional in indoor settings. The sting had been taken out of the viral tail through vaccinations and newer, weaker variants. But Dorothy wasn't taking any chances and continued to wear the washable masks she had bought from Goodwill. She never saw her family of deer on the trail again. They had retreated as people emerged from isolation.

In May, the WHO downgraded the pandemic. "The world's finally out of danger," Dorothy shouted to her husband. "We'll celebrate with a chocolate cake. I'll eat your slice as you won't be able to manage," she laughed.

By late summer, as the garden was awash with deep pink blooms, Dorothy was shocked to hear the statistics. "Hard to believe, Pat. Seven million people died during COVID, but the true number is thought to be three times higher."

Just when she thought the pandemic was ending, the rapid spread of Omicron raised concerns about a new wave of infections, and scientists reported the virus would likely never go away.

"So, COVID's not over after all," Dorothy announced to her husband with a wry smile.

On a sunny morning in early September, Dorothy stared at herself in the vanity mirror. Her mother's face stared back. In that moment, she remembered the Cuban Missile Crisis in 1962, during the Cold War, when all of Britain believed nuclear war was imminent. She recalled climbing the stairs to her mother's flat in a panic and urging her to leave for Ireland.

"I've survived one world war, and I'll survive another," her mother had calmly announced.

As Dorothy stared in the mirror now, she realized that she, too, was a survivor. She had crossed paths with COVID-19, but caution had served as a protective shield.

She made a vow: "I've survived a pandemic, and when the next viral invader attacks, I'll survive that too! Maybe I should get a dog. That'd be way better than talking to a ghost or a mirror." She carried her husband's photo into the living room. "What's Maggie's number? I'm going to bring Donnie home."

Dorothy placed Patrick's photo back on the mantel.

Discovery

LAURIE BROWNE

I have walked in shadow
for too long,
I know,
I hold a picture
in my mind
of how
love could be.
I don't care so much
for what I once
thought necessary.
I won't be fooled
by the glimmer.
I know that sharks
patrol shallow water.

I have learned even waves
that caress
could just as swiftly
pull me under
should I turn my back.

My heart lies among
the discarded
shells and stones
and my edges
have softened
like blue
beach
glass.
Yet still
I shine
and wait
in the light
to be
discovered.

Dorcas in the Dark

CAROLINE KAISER

IT WAS 1984, and it wasn't Big Brother who was watching me—it was Mom. Though I was twenty-one, I was under constant surveillance. She'd stare and she'd hover. I'd hole up in my room and lock the door, but Mom had a key and would barge in, making no excuses.

Being intrusive was just one of many offences she'd stacked up. The first was naming me Dorcas, like she was taking revenge on me for being born. Knowing the psychological scars this name would inflict, Dad had fought tooth and nail against it, but Mom wouldn't give in. Her next big offence was homeschooling me. Dad lost that battle too, so I lost any chance of having a normal social life. And though I devoured every book I could, there were humongous gaps in my education. At least Dad, a doctor, filled me in about science stuff.

Mom, Dad and I lived in a dark, cramped stone cottage in a forest. Our place was so covered in moss and lichen, it looked greenish grey, and you could barely see out the windows because the bushes smothered them. Mom refused to let Dad touch her precious foliage; she'd scold him and slap his hand if she caught him pruning.

My only escape from Mom and the Forest of Gloom was my job. I trudged the half hour into town four days a week to do floral arrangements at Gwendolyn's. I'd trained under Gwen Harper, the soft-spoken owner, and I concentrated on arrangements while she handled everything else. I liked the work, but time felt heavy on my hands when business was slow, which it often was. We were the only florist for miles around, but not enough local people got married or died, so we also sold greeting cards, knick-knacks and souvenirs. We lived in Duckworth, and at Gwendolyn's, you could buy duck paraphernalia to your heart's content.

Greeting any rare tourists to town was a pair of ten-foot-tall grinning mallards. The painted wooden ducks held a sign: Welcome to Duckworth, Where Everything's Ducky! Dad called them Maisie and Marvin. If you drove by and blinked at the wrong moment, it was the worst thing ever—you'd miss the cheesy giant ducks.

Duckworth was full of tired old people. The main drag, Wither Street, included Gwendolyn's, a bank, a library, a drugstore, a grocery store, a smoke shop, a hardware store and a hairdresser's. If you wanted to grab a bite on the four-block strip, your choices were a doughnut shop, a 1950s diner or a dive bar where the town weirdos got drunk and shouted rude remarks at passing girls. Fortunately, Fred's Records, Sure-Footed Shoes, Fantabulous Fabrics and the redundantly named Mimi's Chi-Chi Haute Couture à la Mode saved me from dying of boredom while on Wither Street.

I loved fashion. As Mom had told me many times (as if once wasn't enough), I didn't have much going for me in the looks department, but I decided to make the most of things and dress stylishly. I had nice hazel eyes, but like Dad, I was gangly and had pale, freckled skin—and short red hair, which I gelled to defy gravity. Too bad I had nowhere but work to wear pretty clothes. I didn't really have friends, just acquaintances, and wasn't invited out. That's what happens when you're the quiet girl with the tragic name. Even if I'd been invited to parties, they'd be beer-guzzling bashes where the uniform was sweatshirts and stonewashed jeans—ugh! I'd pop into Mimi's for shoulder duster rhinestone earrings, jewel-toned blazers with padded shoulders, colourful sweaters with batwing sleeves and tapered pants with paper-bag waists. What I couldn't buy, I'd sew myself. At home I'd sketch clothing designs and dream of being a fashion designer in Paris.

One warm Saturday in September, I walked to work through the Forest of Gloom, which always made me claustrophobic. The place was closing in on me; only two tiny patches of blue showed through the treetops. In my sapphire-blue sweater vest, crisp white shirt, grey pencil skirt, blue stockings and silver flats, I was sweating.

Minutes after opening up shop, I spotted Wayne Burrows, who worked at Fred's Records, lingering outside. I hadn't seen him in weeks. Wayne was a rarity in Duckworth—a nice guy. Unlike the town yahoos, he never yelled out "Hey, dork!" when he saw me. He dressed badly—worn jeans, plaid flannel shirts— and had curly blond hair that terminated in the saddest mullet known to mankind, but I could forgive him all that because he always had a smile, a maple-glazed doughnut and cool new music recommendations for me. He'd hang around Gwendolyn's and talk my ear off, leaning across the counter and watching me as I worked. I'd get self-conscious, and a blush would creep into my cheeks. He'd sometimes ask what I was doing on the weekend. Tongue-tied, I'd just shrug and smile. Scraggly hair and fashion crimes aside, he was sweet.

Now Wayne entered Gwendolyn's, and trailing him was a *girl*. I'd never seen him with one before. Was she a girlfriend, or just a friend who was a girl? I soon realized it was Marla May, who did manicures and pedicures out of her parents' basement.

"Hi, Wayne. Marla."

Marla had a big curly perm, wore blue eyeshadow and chomped

gum relentlessly. She also grinned too much, and she was doing it now, reminding me of the ducks. Come to think of it, she was shaped like a duck too. "Hello…*Dorc*-as," she said.

That pause and the stress on that syllable bothered me. So did the fact that she and Wayne were dressed identically—in sickly yellow polo shirts, pleated khakis and penny loafers. And his hair was short. Why had he let her change him into a preppy clone of herself? How could he be so spineless? But what bothered me most was Wayne's worried expression.

Things only got worse when he spoke. Wayne, normally a smooth-as-silk talker, said, "We're getting m-married, and we'll need f-flowers. Won't we…sweetie pie?" Forcing a smile, he gazed at Marla, who gazed back adoringly.

My stomach twitched with nausea. *Why go through with it, Wayne?* "Sure," I said.

"Well, ya might congratulate us!" said Marla.

I took a deep breath and murmured, "Congratulations." I showed them designs from my binder, and we ironed out some details.

Wayne and Marla left, but not before he shot me a hangdog look and mouthed *Sorry*. For the rest of the workday, I beat myself up for being a pathetic loser. When Wayne had asked what I was doing on the weekend all those times, why hadn't I whispered "What do you have in mind?" and smiled flirtatiously? I'd failed to show the slightest bit of interest in him. Now that Marla had him in her clutches, he'd never show his face at Gwendolyn's again. I'd miss him. Maybe we would've only ever been friends and never dated, but the point was, I could've *tried*.

By the time I got home, I was in no mood to cope with Mom. I rushed to my bedroom, put some Echo and the Bunnymen on the turntable and cranked up the volume.

Within seconds, my door flew open. "Dorcas Dearbourne, stop this racket and get out here immediately!" Even Ian

McCulloch's soaring, angst-filled vocals couldn't drown out Mom's piercing voice.

I groaned and lowered the volume. "What? What is it?"

Mom's face, with its beady black eyes and sour mouth, confronted me. She was wearing a circa-1967 flowery housedress, and her curlers were covered with a filmy kerchief. She actually went out in public like that. How was it possible I was even related to this person?

"Set the table."

"I will if you ask politely." I lingered in the doorway.

Dad hovered behind her. "Be *nice*, Joy."

She ignored him. "Dorcas, turn the Funny Men off and get out here."

Dad snickered. "They're called Echo and the Bunnymen. And hey, I kind of like those guys." He winked at me, and I burst out laughing.

"Shut your trap, Henry." Mom raised an eyebrow. "Dorcas? You're coming?"

I sighed. "All right."

I set the table as Mom plunked down food on it. A hunk of pink corned beef, gluey mashed potatoes and boiled-into-mush broccoli. When we all sat down, she asked me, "So what's with you?"

"I lost a friend today, Mom. And I maybe could've done something about that."

"Wayne?" asked Dad, and I nodded. "Aw, I'm sorry, honey."

Mom shook her head. "If only you'd curb that tongue of yours, Dorcas."

I smacked my hand down on the table. "Jesus Christ, Mom! It wasn't like that. It was what I *didn't* say. And stop using my name. I hate my name."

"Control yourself. It's an elegant name. It's from the Greek for 'gazelle,' you know. Your great-grandmother was named Dorcas."

We'd had this conversation before. "Exactly—it's ancient. And those jerks who call me a dork don't know what it means."

"I never should've allowed that name." Dad squeezed my hand.

I nodded. "Yeah. If name is destiny, I'm freaking *doomed*."

"Oh, stop being so dramatic! A name doesn't set you up for success or failure. Decide what you want to do with your life and just do it," Mom said.

"I *have* decided. I've told you a million times—I want to be a fashion designer, but you don't support me."

"Dorcas, why would I? It's a pipe dream. Pick something practical, for heaven's sake."

"Stop calling me Dorcas!"

That was it—enough was enough. Trembling, I stood up and shoved aside my chair. "I won't listen to this garbage. And I'm not putting up with you anymore. I'm going to make something of myself, and I can't do it in Duckworth. I'm going to the city."

Her eyes wide, Mom shot up from her seat and flung her napkin to the floor. "No! You are not! I've already lost one daughter to that godforsaken place—I won't lose you too."

Dad said, "Karen comes home all the time, Joy. You didn't *lose* her. And if you smarten up, maybe you won't lose Dorcas."

Karen had twelve years on me, had escaped years ago and was working as a nurse in the city. She visited us faithfully, even though Mom treated her as shabbily as she treated me.

Mom's fury ebbed away, and she slumped into her seat. After making sure she'd caught my eye, she held my gaze and released an ear-shattering wail. How fake! *Nice try, Mom.*

I rolled my eyes. "This is messed up. I'm getting out of here. Now. I can't take it anymore."

Dad and I fled to my bedroom to pack my things.

"Can I drive you to Aunt Shelley's?" he asked. "She'll let you stay until you find your feet." Shelley was Dad's sister and a cool pottery teacher who lived in this tiny yellow-brick Victorian house.

"Perfect."

"Got any money?"

"I've been saving up," I said. "Let's stop at the bank."

He pulled a thick wad of bills from his wallet and pushed it into my hand. "Here's more."

"Aw, thanks, Dad." Then a painful thought stabbed me. "Oh, I need to stop by Gwen's house and give her two weeks' notice." I'd take the train in for my final couple of weeks.

After Dad called Aunt Shelley and we finished packing, we hauled everything downstairs. Mom was sipping tea from a dainty teacup.

I said softly, "Mom? I'm leaving now."

She snapped to attention and her glare shifted from me to Dad. "And *you're* helping her? Well, go on, both of you—get out!" She hurled the cup against the wall.

Without another word, we left, and Dad heaved my overstuffed suitcase and some boxes into the car.

We hit the road, got cash from the ATM and stopped at Gwen's. At my news, she tearfully hugged me. "What'll I do without you?" Soon, though, her mood brightened. "Actually…this might be just the push I've needed. I've been thinking of shutting down here and setting up shop in the city. What do you say? Want to work for me?"

I grinned. "Of course!"

"Let's talk about it later."

I nodded. Besides Karen and Aunt Shelley, Gwen would be a familiar someone in an unfamiliar place. Part of me was petrified to move to the city, frightened of the newness of it all. The other part couldn't wait to see how my life would change. Yeah, I'd still work for Gwen, but I could take fashion design courses at the college.

On the drive out of town, I blew a farewell kiss to the giant ducks and narrated the sorry saga of Wayne and Marla. Then I got wistful. "Dad, I'll miss you. And I hate to abandon you to Mom." I paused. "So why have you stayed with her, exactly?"

"Well, I'm used to her."

I shook my head. "*Seriously?* That's so lame."

"I couldn't abandon you to *her*. No way would she have allowed me full custody of you without starting a war, and the courts always favour mothers. So I stuck around to mitigate her damage. I figured that having one full-time parent who loved you would be better for you than hardly ever seeing me."

"You wanted to leave her?"

"In the last few years, every single goddamn day."

"But you stayed because of me?"

"That's right, kiddo." He squeezed my shoulder. "And I don't regret it for a moment."

"But Dad, I'm an adult now, and I'm leaving. You don't have to be there anymore." I had a sudden inspiration. "Hey, let's get a place together!"

He chuckled. "As good as that sounds, it's time you were on your own. Don't be like your mother—follow your heart's desire in this life. Change your name to one you love. Find a guy who's not such a gutless wonder that he can't even work up the courage to ask you out."

I sagged at his words. Yeah, I wanted to do all that, but what about Dad? He couldn't remain shackled to Mom for eternity. Without me there, he'd be the sole target of her explosive rage.

"But what'll you do?" I asked.

"Oh, don't you worry about me. I'll be fine." His smile was sly, like he was keeping the world's biggest secret but dying to reveal it.

I couldn't stand the suspense, so just like an old-time movie detective I said, "C'mon, spill it."

"While you're getting settled at Shelley's, I'll be house hunting in the city. And looking for office space. Honey, we'll see each other as much as you like."

I squealed, then flung my arms around Dad with such force, he nearly lost control of the wheel.

He was laughing, and so was I.

Alignment

LAURA WYTHE

"YOU SCREAMED AT me, Sarah." They were on the Trans-Canada Highway, hours out of the Sault, and still no sign of Wawa. He was trying to keep them both awake, even if it meant arguing. "You hit the van so hard with your fist you could have damaged it. You said we had to go—or something bad would happen. And so, I listened. Not an ideal time to leave, four o'clock in the afternoon, peak traffic on Wonderland Road. Everyone else heading home, lucky them. But I listened, and here we are hours later in the rain and it's taking forever."

Sarah twisted her long fine hair between her fingers, ran her fingers down and gave a hard tug, pulling out a thin hank of dark roving. Her eyes were bright blue lasers focused on a point in space. "It's the alignment. Jupiter with Uranus on one side and Neptune on the other."

"We shouldn't be going west. No one will want us during a pandemic."

It was early spring and almost midnight. The rain was getting worse. Sarah drove accordingly, slowing and speeding up, making it harder for him to tell if she was falling asleep. Suddenly, she veered off the road at a sign, but not a big sign, like for a park, and so he missed it.

"I remember this place," she told him. "I was here one summer and crawled out to see the rock paintings. There should be parking. We can't stay on the highway all night in this weather."

The van slewed down a steep gravel slope. Rain had formed ice on the snow; gullies and trees hemmed them in. The rain slapped the trees around them, sending cascades of water across the windshield; the wipers frenzied. She slowed to a steady crawl as she negotiated the slope and the curves. Down, down they drove into darker and darker forest.

"There!" He pointed to an opening on the left. A parking lot, he thought.

"We should go further. This isn't it."

"Oh no, Sarah, let's wait for morning to explore. We don't know what the road is like, especially after the winter."

She turned left onto what was really a gravel pad for turning around on the hillside, and parked so the van faced the way out. This bit of space in the forest, strangely, made him feel more vulnerable. *Easier for alien abduction, huh?* It was a dark thought, but not an obsession. The obsessed one was Sarah.

Sarah stared into the rain, as she had been for hours looking for the lines on the road. "Can you feel it?"

"I feel tired." Sorry, too, that he'd agreed to the rushed exit from his parents' house in Westmount, where they'd been staying under growing parental scrutiny, neither of them working now. Neither of them had worked much in the last year, anyway, since she'd lost her job with the government. They'd been criss-crossing the country, picking up work, losing it, returning home to crash with whichever family member would take them in. When the pandemic struck, his parents took them in again. This trip, there would be no seasonal work, nothing but closed doors ahead of them.

Sarah's hands moved from side to side along the top of the

steering wheel. He checked to see if the van was really in park, the brake on. Her voice was soft, certain. "You must feel the energy."

He half-joked, "Yeah, this place is creepy." He wanted to take the keys from the ignition but instead, he reached out to take her closest hand, his so much larger than hers. He focused on the physical, what could be seen and touched. She let her fingers lie limp in his. The creaking branches on the trees overhead could crash down—if not on them, then onto the road, blocking their way out. The heavy rain fell pell-mell down the gravel track, pooling into shiny puddles that followed the tracks where she had driven in then swung the van around to park. He'd watched the rear lights glow in the black night as she backed closer and closer to a drop-off. He'd held his breath until she stopped, and if it had been daylight, he'd have jumped out to check how close she'd parked. How far behind them was the drop?

Sarah was always making statements, like they were dares, or a truth. Like she was trying to frighten him out of his skin. Last year, they'd taken a trail that turned out to be miles long, no phone or flashlight, late in the day. She'd pulled him to come with her when they should have been having a beer and some food. It was madness. Not *H-angry* but what he'd labelled *cH-razy*, like how this trip started. They ended up on a rocky lookout a few hours later, just as the sun set. Beautiful view: nothing but trees and hills forever. The moon rose. He got goosebumps as she talked about all the humans that had been there before them. A place of sacrifice. A place where wolves gathered. He was ready to howl, to jump himself. She had stood back from the cliff edge in the shadows, watching him. Her voice from the darkness: "I guess we'll have to spend the night and see what happens."

Ah, this "tempting fate" thing she had. His heart had remained in his chest, his running shoes planted on the bedrock, toes curled up inside. He hadn't even turned around, just said, "Listen, you know this trail. You know the way. Let's go down now."

"It's getting too dark."

"There's a trail marker somewhere. You better find it."

Once the cliff was behind them, he actually enjoyed the moonlit walk back to their campsite. The trail back had followed an old road.

Tonight, there was no full moon to guide them. On the flipside, he was safely locked inside the van, and he wasn't getting out.

"Can't you feel it?" She was starting up on the spirit stuff again. "I feel a presence."

He tossed her a blanket and took one for himself. "Let's get some sleep." He stretched his legs out. He could fall asleep anywhere.

They were peering into the windows of the van, peering at him. Not aliens. Tall figures, three of them, moose-high but on two legs, dressed in hide or bark with woven stuff sticking out, and masks—or were they faces? It was difficult to say whether they were human, animal, or weirdly, tree? Carefully he drew his socked feet up onto the seat and wrapped his arms around his legs. *Do not make eye contact,* he thought. *Do not look them in the eye. Don't look at them at all. They seem real, but they are not.* They were staring at him with something akin to gentle curiosity. Pixies and elves, he'd heard they could be vindictive. And trolls hated you if you tried to cross their waterways. Yet here these things were—something from the land, something you didn't normally see, like she'd called them up, or they'd been called to this place from a thousand kilometres away.

"Can you see them, too?"

He didn't blink, didn't answer. Where was she leading him? Into her great angst? All the drama, but maybe it was a deep depression, a death wish. Maybe he was sharing a psychotic episode? Fuck it! It was his father all over again. The ghosts or beasts or shamans in masks—or trees—were moving around the van now, gazing into all the windows. Looking for hunting gear, maybe? He said nothing to her. Gently, he closed his eyes, pictured the creature-beings, and said in his thoughts, *We didn't mean to disturb you. I feel like we interrupted something.* He saw the circular turnaround, understood that it was their sacred place—a small wound on the hillside that needed to be watched. *Please guide us out and onto our journey. We wish you only good.*

A sense of conferring on his side of the van, under the drip line of the trees. They felt the van should be removed, but the humans were welcome. After all, it was rare for humans to occupy this space at such an auspicious time. Or maybe the time hadn't come yet— he questioned his reading—and the creatures were trying to figure out where to keep him and Sarah until such a day. How the hell could he know? He and Sarah could be skeletons when the back roads opened up properly. Shit, how much of Sarah's desire was informing their conference? He had to be clear it wasn't a negotiation. *I'm not interested in or afraid of you, and the woman with me won't be staying either,* he thought. *She will follow me.*

The conferring paused.

"Sarah, I think maybe we disturbed something." He checked his phone for the time. They'd been asleep for over four hours. "Sarah, I'm awake now. Let's trade seats and I'll drive."

He had the tone right—firm and friendly, not condescending. Matter of fact. Like asking her to move over to her own side of the bed. Her body over his as she traded seats, all the while staring into the dark to where he'd felt the things were. The van started. The rain had lightened to a mist and the deep grooves in the road were easy enough to straddle. He pulled around each twist in the road and didn't stop when he saw the pavement ahead, just turned onto the highway. All clear. A nod and thanks to the spirits back there.

The road ahead was empty, only a half-moon sailing past Jupiter among high wispy clouds. He was miles from home, still heading the wrong way.

Summer's End

DONNA COSTA

Cardinal overhead pings the ocean
of foliage searching for
the enemy.

Time.

Siren in the distance groans the pain
of the ambulance's occupant.
OH-oh OH-oh OH-OOOOh.

I sit beside the dead
nettle and mint
as ants crawl on orange halves
by the waterspout
green with algae
and age.

Where is the oriole the orange was meant to attract?

Thorny blackberry canes sprawl
uncontrolled uncontained
unsettled.

Vehicle traffic mimics waves
lapping cement shores.

Listen. Listen.

Clothesline pulley, idle, silent
repurposed for feathered friends.
Or foes.
Tall white garden-phlox
with bleeding eyes.
Tiny ant on my forearm scurries
to avoid the finger flick
over the edge.
Its final fall.

Inevitable.
Surely it knows?

Listen. Listen.

Lulling waves of traffic rhythm
lap my shores.

Cardinal stops its pinging.
Hummingbird feeder

empty of sweet
nectar.

Oriole sings a parting song.

Grandpa's Harvest

TRUDY CLOUDT

ERIC HEARD THE phone ring in the kitchen as Mom unlocked the side door. *It's probably for her, she can get it.* He shifted positions on the living room couch. The truth of the matter was he found it extremely difficult to get up and move these days—he just felt heavy and hopeless. This had nothing to do with his size, it was everything else; school, friends, his future. It all just seemed so bleak.

Thump went Mom's school bag, and then footsteps scurried across the kitchen floor. *She's always in such a rush!* "Hi Dad," he heard Mom say; she sounded a little out of breath.

He could hear his grandpa on the other end. "What took you so long to answer de phone? Tell Eric to be *ready*, I need his help with de garden tomorrow. Seven o'clock, I be dere."

Eric watched his mom scampering around the kitchen. She'd only been home a few minutes and was already chopping vegetables for supper.

"Eric, Grandpa needs your help at the cottage."

"Yeah Mom, I heard, Grandpa has two settings, remember? Loud and louder."

"He has trouble gauging his volume since he lost his hearing. It will be good for you to be in the fresh air—besides, Grandpa really appreciates your help."

"Yeah," Eric shrugged.

"I'm so relieved you'll be unplugged from that stupid *World of Warcraft*. It's taking way too much of your time, and then you're too exhausted for school, where it really counts!"

Oh Jeez, here she goes, winding herself up again.

"You worry too much, Mom!"

"Eric, you have everything going for you. You're intelligent and talented, you just need a plan and perseverance."

"I *have* a plan," he said as he thumped down the stairs into the dark cavern of the family room to log on. *Of course, she's going to say that stuff, she's my mother—it's what they all say, even when the kid's a big loser. She should save that positive pep talk for her classroom, I'm fifteen, not a little kid.*

"As soon as I figure out how to disconnect the computer," she called down after him, "we'll get this under control. I can't stand to see you waste time caught up in some imaginary universe."

"Yeah, right Mom."

Then as soon as she needs the computer for her report cards, she'll be in panic mode and I'll have to put it together again.

Seven o'clock came early the next morning. Eric knew that Grandpa did not take no for an answer. He knew better than to protest or say he had better things to do. Grandpa flickered the headlights as Eric pulled his dark hoodie over his head and stuffed his feet into his sneakers. The handle felt cold as he opened the vehicle door.

Grandpa's fine-lined ruddy complexion was a reminder of the years he'd spent working outside. He looked ready to put in a full day's work in his flannel shirt and steel-toed boots. Erik smiled when he noticed the razor-sharp crease that Grandma insisted on ironing into Grandpa's trousers.

"Hi Eric, are you ready to work in de garden?"

"Yeah."

He flopped onto the back seat of Grandpa's warm van and was lulled to sleep by the steady rhythm of the tires on the country roads.

In seventy minutes, Eric lurched forward as Grandpa slammed on the brakes. "Come on Eric, time to get to work."

The cool, fresh air from Grandpa's open door reminded him that there was no snooze button within reach. He rubbed his eyes, gave himself a little shake and propelled himself into the early morning. *Grandpa is the only person in the world who thinks driving to the cottage at seven in the morning on a Saturday is fun. Just because he learned how to plant a garden when he was a kid in the Netherlands doesn't mean I have to. He should get with the times and go to the grocery store like everyone else. Hhhhhh! Might as well get this over with!*

They were an odd pair as they made their way to the garden: Grandpa, sturdy and compact, Eric taller and agile. Both had the same fashion sense when it came to pants, however. Eric thought of it as "gangsta" style, crotch to the knees. For Grandpa, it was more comfortable to fasten his belt under his belly and allow his loose pants to succumb to gravity. Their stride had an uncanny resemblance; there was harmony between the grandfather and his grandson.

Eric looked up to Grandpa as a strong male that he could count on after his parents divorced. He knew that Grandpa's love for him was fierce, and he loved Grandpa back.

Steam rose from their breath as they made their way to the tool shed. The early morning light dappled through trees and glistened off dewy blades of grass. A peaceful place, but active with sounds of nature. They were accompanied on their walk by birds, chipmunks and red squirrels. Eric cocked his ear to hear the waves break on the beach below. He took a deep breath and allowed his lungs to fill with oxygen-rich air. He felt a little less heavy and a little less burdened.

Grandpa's thick, calloused hands manoeuvred the padlock of the tool shed. With a flick of the light switch, the reclaimed dining room chandelier cast a warm glow over bundles of rope, shovels, rakes and spades. Eric looked around and saw scaffolding that Grandpa had used in his carpentry work, sawhorses textured with deep rivets and grooves, hammers, toolboxes and nails. The shed walls were thick with neatly organized devices and implements. Many of them paid tribute to the work he did in building his life in Canada and in turn, building up his adopted country.

Grandpa instructed, while Eric retrieved the necessary tools and placed them methodically by the garden.

"My knees are so stiff dis morning Eric, it's arthritis, I just can't move like I used to." The old man lowered himself onto a tree stump at the edge of the garden and rubbed his knees. "I was young once too, you know, like you."

Eric chuckled at the thought. His mind could not imagine his grandpa as anything but old, and himself as anything but young.

"It's okay Grandpa, I've got this." Eric stood tall and gave Grandpa a fist pump.

He felt good that his grandpa needed him.

"Grandpa, what are those window frames for?" asked Eric.

"Oh, dey are fence posts to hold up de chicken wire to keep de rabbits out!" said Grandpa. "No use throwing anything away when you can reuse it!"

"Yeah," replied Eric with a shrug. *If you say so.*

Grandpa's instructions were direct and to the point. "You have to turn de soil and break it up real fine, so de tiny shoots can find der way to de sunlight." Eric responded with his shovel, and released dark, rich earth from the scarred crust left by the frosty grip of winter. Eric breathed in the heady fragrance of newly turned soil.

They worked in tandem. Grandpa delivered the same instructions he had heard at the lips of his father and grandfather in Dutch, decades ago and an ocean away. Eric's young body and open mind provided the means for the work to be done.

"First, we mark de rows with string, Eric. We have to make sure de rows are straight and true. Take de time dat you need, don't rush. If you're going to do something, you might as well do it right." Eric strummed the string to test for tautness. "Have a clear focus in life Eric, and decide on de best path. Once you've made your mind up, don't stop until you're finished!"

Eric felt good around Grandpa, just the two of them. He liked the way Grandpa spoke and the feel of the breeze from the lake against his face.

"Now, beans, dey need a little more room between dem to grow, and plant dem two together, dey need a friend," said Grandpa. "Choose your friends wisely. Don't hang around with de foolish guys, Eric, it's a waste of time."

"De lettuce, you put a lot of seeds in, because as you use it, more can grow. You can't use what you don't plant, you know."

Eric seeded the lettuce generously.

"Work hard at school Eric, try to get de most out of it. You can be anything you want to be, you know, just put your mind to it!"

"Hmm," replied Eric.

"Now de little plants, dey reach for the sun, dey don't worry dey can't do it! You have to believe in yourself Eric, and always do your best. You will surprise yourself with what you can accomplish."

Eric wiped away wetness on his cheek.

He followed the instructions, knowing it was easier that way; besides, Grandpa knew a lot about gardening and about what each little seed needed to thrive. "Also, Eric, weeds always grow. It's really important to get rid of dem when dey are small. Make wise choices, so dey don't take over and ruin your garden or your life."

Eric thought about the amount of time he spent in front of the computer, going on imaginary quests in imaginary worlds, eating imaginary food.

Grandpa and Eric worked that day until the golden sun dipped below the horizon of the rhythmic waves of Lake Huron. The glorious sun bid good night, offering a dynamic splendour of light to everything in its wake. The wise grandfather and his teenage grandson worked as silhouettes against the backdrop of the spectacular sky. Their independent forms moved together, forming one strong purposeful shape united by interest and intent, and then eased apart again, each retaining his nuanced individuality. This was repeated until the garden and the lessons were rooted firmly.

Grandpa and Eric stood back to inspect their work. They had planted a garden that was like no other. Before them, neatly spaced rows were marked by recycled wood and branches. Copper plumbing pipes formed arched structures for pole beans, strings hung down for the growing plants to grasp. Rabbits were barred by chicken wire and window-frame fence posts.

"We did a good job, Eric!" said Grandpa. Eric smiled. "Pretty soon we'll have more vegetables than we can use and enough to share! If you have a garden, dere is always enough to go around. One of de secrets to a happy life is to share what you can."

While the ride up had been quiet and peaceful, lulling Eric to sleep, the drive home was lively. Eric and Grandpa shared a love of good music. Grandpa popped in a cassette tape, and cranked up the volume to make up for his hearing loss. What better way to drive home than to the sounds of ABBA? Eric chuckled as he pulled his hoodie over his ears and closed his eyes. *At least it's not polka music.*

Eric knew that gardening was not a single event, but rather a season. Many Saturdays in his youth began with Grandpa flickering his headlights at seven in the morning and him falling into the van. *Jeez, why can't Grandpa just be normal and go golfing or something. At a normal time. Without me!*

Eric learned how to discern the crops from the weeds, and he realized that Grandpa was right about how easy it would be to let the weeds overtake the garden and lose sight of the crops.

"You know Eric, you have to make sure to stay away from drugs, drinking and bad influences. Dey will only make you miserable."

"Yeah, I know."

"Now I want to show you something Eric, it's really *important*," said Grandpa in earnest. "I want you to turn around." From the clearing near the garden, Eric turned around. "What do you see?"

"Well, it's the cottage in the forest."

"Did you know dat we started each one of dose trees in de vegetable garden at home, Eric? When we bought dis property, dere was not one tree on it, just like de farmer's fields, no trees! De trees dat you see, dey were only de size of your thumb."

Eric looked at his thumb.

"Grandma and I planted those treelings and took care of dem until dey were ready to be planted here."

"Wow Grandpa, you're kidding."

"No, I am not! If you have a good idea, trust it, take care of it and watch it grow. Many people thought I was crazy and it would never work."

"It sure did work, Grandpa!"

"Yes, Eric, and your goals will work too. You have to believe in yourself, never give up! See, from a little idea, Eric, you can grow a forest! I did, and I'm no one special."

"Hm," said Eric. *That's what you think.*

The next year was a milestone for Grandpa and Grandma, the year of their sixtieth wedding anniversary. Grandpa was trying to convince Grandma that they should put an announcement and picture in the paper. The family planned a wonderful, weekend-long celebration at the cottage.

In early spring, with Eric's help, the garden went in as usual. Grandpa struggled to breathe the hot, humid air; he had developed COPD.

On celebration day, the family swarmed out of their vehicles and made a beeline to the garden.

"Wow, this is not up to Grandpa's standards, we'd better get to work," said Eric. "Quick, pull the weeds, luckily Grandpa moves slow."

"Which ones are weeds?" asked his young cousin.

Finally, Grandpa made it over. The family had finished their feeble rescue attempt and they looked at each other sheepishly. Grandpa shook his head with a look of disappointment.

"Yeah, yeah, it looks okay."

This was the last time Grandpa went to his garden at the cottage. He spent the rest of the summer in his recliner at home. His oxygen mask was always within arm's reach.

"It's really hard to grow old. I can't do anything anymore. I just feel hopeless!"

Eric helped Grandpa with his oxygen mask. *I don't want Grandpa to feel like a loser, that's the worst feeling ever!*

"Eric, don't forget to plant the garlic so it will come up in the spring."

Eric wiped his eyes.

In November, unexpectedly and on his own terms, Grandpa passed away.

The following spring, Eric and Mom knew what to do. They stood in front of the garden patch, tools and implements in hand, seeds ready to go.

"Okay Eric, do you want to till the patch? I'll unroll the chicken wire."

"You know, Mom, I don't feel right planting the garden without Grandpa."

"I was thinking the same thing, Eric—this was his space, his garden, his passion. Maybe we'll feel differently next year."

Eric nodded.

The following year the plot became a pile of debris from the leaves. There was no garden.

A few years later, Eric started to plant some seeds of change in his life. He moved to a place of his own and found he no longer had time for computer games. He cultivated a plan to upgrade his sciences with the goal of becoming a healthcare professional. He met a lovely young lady who encouraged his vision.

In time, he married that woman of his dreams and became a mental health nurse, where he shared his knowledge and drew from his experience to help others. That spring, Eric planted a garden. Eric's garden was masterfully tended and his harvest was plentiful.

incandescent

KRISTA CARSON

i'm hazy, fetal

in this river
of bedsheets.

as i enter
my electric pain,

i am inward—
migraine.

until promises
of honey light beckon

and i unfurl
myself, wild—

a soft, crazy petal.

Maude's Chance

CHRISTINE LANGLOIS

WHEN MAUDE HEARD Albert creep into their room at dawn after his night shift, she leaped out of bed and turned up the kerosene lamp. Before he could pull off his jacket, she started in, whispering so she didn't wake Sarah.

"There's a typhoid outbreak here! The nurse told me."

Albert set his lunch pail on the bureau. "That's not good." But he didn't sound shocked.

"Did you know?"

"Some guys have been talking."

"I wish you'd warned me."

"You're already scared of everything. I didn't want to make it worse."

"The worst is that she's opened a sickroom right across the hall. Here—in the boarding house. Albert, do you think we should leave?"

He ran his hand through his dark hair grey with rock dust. "Whoa! Nobody's leaving. I just got on at the mine."

"But typhoid's deadly. What if Sarah caught it?"

Albert pressed his lips into a thin line and shook his head.

His voice was even but Maude could tell he was losing patience. "Maude, you watch that child like a mama bear. And that's admirable. But she's strong and healthy for such a little thing, and so are we. We're not living in some shack taking our water out of a stream. We're in a respectable boarding house with clean water. Your nurse friend even said so. We'll be fine!"

"But…"

"Maude, my answer is no." He spoke slowly, emphasizing each word. "It took a lot to get here. Men are making fortunes in Cobalt. I am not giving up at the first sign of trouble."

Albert turned and started to undress. She tried one more time. "Then, maybe I should take Sarah back south myself. Just for the winter. Violet said it's going to be bad." Maude didn't say the rest—that Violet expected so many patients that she was offering Maude a job to help her.

Maude jumped when Albert's fist hit the bureau top. Then he shouted at her, which he seldom did. "I said no! We've decided to live here now!"

You decided.

Sarah sat up crying. Maude reached over and patted her back to sleep as Albert squeezed his large frame past her to crawl into bed. Maude perched on the edge of the bed to wait the hour until she could take Sarah down for breakfast. She ignored the creak of bedsprings coming through the thin walls as other boarders rose. She wished she'd never set eyes on this godforsaken place. And now she couldn't leave.

"Can I just go say good morning?" Sarah whined for the third time. The six-year-old stared across the boarding house dining hall at the only other woman in the room—the nurse, Violet, dressed in her spotless white uniform, alone with her coffee. All around them were miners hunched over their plates, talking in loud voices and shovelling food into their mouths.

"I said no, Sarah."

Sarah rested her chin on her upturned hand and sulked. The six-year-old had been enamoured with the nurse from the first day they'd met in the hall. Maude had been, too. The nurse had admired Sarah's red curls and blue eyes—"just like your mama's"—and given her a mint. She'd reassured Maude that the water their landlady was offering for sale was safe. Then Violet started joining her and Sarah at breakfast on days when Albert was on nights and sleeping. Maude had never had a friend like Violet—a New Woman with a job and her own money. Violet made her feel modern.

But that all changed when Violet had confided in her about the typhoid outbreak and broached the subject of a job.

Maude was terrified at the thought—typhoid! She didn't want Violet to know, so she kept talking. "How can you care for them in the boarding house?"

"They can pay for care, and the landlady and I are happy to oblige. Nobody wants to get quarantined in a pest house without any help. It's a death sentence."

"There are pest houses in Cobalt?"

"There are now—the mines are opening them. But patients who can pay are looking for beds. That's why I'm hiring." The nurse's voice was full of confidence and pride. "And I would train you. I'm fully experienced in germ theory."

Maude demurred. She told Violet that Albert didn't want her to work. But really, she couldn't imagine doing work that was so dangerous. When she and Sarah got back to their room, she made sure they both washed their hands with lye soap. What if the woman was contagious?

This morning, she chose a different table and avoided eye contact when Violet came in. As she poked at her food, Maude went over last night's argument with Albert. How would she change his mind?

"Mama? You're not listening!" Maude looked up at Sarah. "Are we going to the shops today?"

"Yes, and maybe the train station." She'd inquire about the cost of two tickets. Just the idea made her hands go clammy. She'd never crossed her husband and didn't have any money of her own to leave anyway. But she couldn't think of anything else to do.

A mine whistle blew long and high. "That means another accident," Sarah said.

"Yes." Maude now knew the sound well. It happened every few days. Each mine had its own number of whistles, so rescuers would know where to head when the alarm was raised. She'd only ever heard four whistles—for the tiny Smith mine.

At the second whistle, the usual roar in the dining hall quieted down as most of the men listened too, except for a couple of new arrivals who kept talking loudly.

When the fourth rang out, Maude looked over at the handful of Smith miners in the room. She felt sorry for the exhausted men starting to push away from their table, but then there was a fifth whistle and Maude saw the relief in their faces as they relaxed back into their chairs.

Sarah leaned over. "Mama, how many is that?"

"That's five, honey." And then there was a sixth whistle.

"What's Papa's number?"

"It's nine but don't worry. It won't be Coniagas."

Seven.

Eight. Maude could hear her heartbeat thudding in her ears.

"Mama, Papa's number is next," Sarah said in a tiny voice squeaky with fear.

Nine.

Maude held her breath, willing the whistle to sound again.

"One more, please, one more," she whispered to herself. But the seconds passed in silence until it was clear the accident was at Coniagas.

"Let's go," someone shouted. The room erupted with scraping

chairs and thudding boots as miners grabbed their coats and ran for the door.

"Mama, it's nine. It's nine!"

Albert. Albert was down there. Maude grabbed Sarah's hand and followed the miners out the front door. Ahead of her on the road, rescuers loped toward the mine, their open jackets flapping like the wings of giant birds. Behind them, a few women followed. Maude and Sarah ran to catch up. Every few minutes, they stepped off the dirt track as teams of horses pulling ore carts thundered past in a swirl of dust. A constant banging grew louder as they headed up a long hill toward the distinctive outline of a head frame poking above a stand of jack pine.

"What's that noise?" Sarah asked.

"I think it's called the concentrator," Maude said. She'd never been on a mine property before.

At the top of the hill, a man leaned out of a small guardhouse and waved them through. Everyone broke into a run and Maude encouraged Sarah to go faster. They passed a large tent on a wooden platform with a small sign above the door—*Pest House*. A heavy wooden bar blocked the exit from the outside. She pulled Sarah closer and moved toward a knot of women standing in the mine yard watching the shaft entrance.

A shout came from the front of the crowd. "They're bringing men up!"

"Can you see Papa?" Sarah asked, jumping up and down to see between the adults.

Maude looked hard at the dirty faces of the four men who had been rescued. Covered in rock dust from their helmets to their boots, they all looked the same. One of them was as tall as Albert. But then another woman called his name and he turned to her with a wave.

"No, honey."

Sarah started to cry.

With every arrival of the shaft bucket, more miners walked free, a few into the arms of waiting wives. By nightfall, Maude and Sarah were among only a handful of women in the yard. A half-moon rose in the lavender sky. Maude sat in the dirt and Sarah huddled in her lap for warmth. The child had stopped asking for food. No one spoke.

Maude fixed her eyes on the moon to empty her mind of unbidden images. Albert buried alive under jagged rocks. Rescuers walking right past him. Albert surviving but his body broken. If Albert didn't…she would have to… But no words came next.

"Maude!" She looked up to see the nurse, Violet, standing over her in a long, dark nurse's cape against the evening chill.

Maude scrambled to her feet. "Have you heard anything?"

"No. The mine doctor summoned me. He expects he'll need assistance soon." Violet pointed to an older man standing near the entrance to the shaft.

The squeal of the winch announced that another bucket had reached the surface. "Got an injury here," a rescuer yelled.

Maude grabbed Sarah and rushed forward. She could make out only lighted helmets and dark figures until a lantern lit up the men's faces. One of them was Albert, held up between two others and grimacing in pain. She pushed closer.

"Where was he struck?" Violet shouted to the rescuers as they set Albert down on a stretcher.

"Head, shoulders," one rescuer called as he turned to go back.

Maude reached the stretcher and gasped. She tried to shield Sarah but the girl squirmed away.

"Your head's hurt, Papa!"

Albert's face was streaked with dirt and dark blood that seeped from matted hair on the side of his head. His left shoulder sloped oddly. His body trembled but he was conscious.

She leaned closer. "Oh, Albert! I was so…"

The doctor, now wearing a mask, elbowed between them. "Back up, ma'am! We'll take care of him."

Maude pulled Sarah away as the doctor cut off Albert's torn shirt to examine his scraped chest and shoulder.

"Dislocated shoulder," he said. "Chest rash." He looked over at Violet and she nodded. "Head wound needs sutures but not deep. Left ankle sprained, possible fracture."

Maude took a ragged breath. *He isn't going to die.* She hugged Sarah close so that she couldn't watch as Violet and the doctor reset Albert's shoulder. Albert screamed and the girl shuddered. The doctor bandaged Albert's ankle and left to attend to another injured miner, leaving Violet to close the head wound. In a few minutes the nurse was tying off the last stitch. Albert looked over at Sarah and winked.

"Now we can all go home!" the girl said.

Violet turned around at that. Above her mask, her eyes were steely.

"I'm sorry, Maude. The doctor should have told you. Albert has the typhoid rash on his chest. He has to be quarantined."

Maude pulled back from Sarah. "Violet, no!"

"What!" Albert shouted.

Violet nodded to two men. One quickly pulled a strap across Albert's chest. They lifted the stretcher and walked off. Violet followed them.

Maude ran beside the stretcher. "Albert, what should I...?"

"Mama, make Papa come back!" Sarah called from behind, her voice shrill.

Maude stopped to go back to Sarah. She screamed into the dark after Violet. "Tell me where you're taking him." But she knew where—the Pest House.

Hidden in the shadows on the other side of the road, Maude watched as Violet removed the wooden bar and led the stretcher bearers through the door of the white tent which glowed with lights inside. Maude waited a few minutes until the men left carrying the empty stretcher, then she guided Sarah across the road.

"Stay here. I'm going to find Papa. Promise me you won't move." Sarah nodded and shrunk back against the outside of the tent.

Maude ripped a length of fabric off the hem of her dress, tied it around her face and slipped through the door.

Inside the tent, a string of electric lights illuminated two rows of high beds made of rough-sawn wood on either side of a central aisle. Groaning men lay sprawled on each bed. One man—a boy, really—retched into a bucket. She gagged at the smell of vomit and feces and turned to go back. Then she remembered that Albert was one of these doomed men, and she turned again and kept going. Violet was guiding her husband onto the last open bed. His face was slack with despair.

Maude called to him. When he saw her, his expression registered surprise, relief and then fear. "Lovey! You can't be in here!"

Violet let go of Albert and ran up the aisle toward her. "You're not allowed!"

Maude stood her ground. "I'm taking him back to the boarding house—to your sickroom. I'm accepting that job you offered."

"That's brave, but…"

"Maude, I won't allow it," Albert yelled. "It's too dangerous."

"And I won't allow you to stop me." Her voice caught. "I love you. I won't let you die in a pest house. If I can help it."

"But what about Sarah? We'd never forgive ourselves."

"I can care for you and keep Sarah safe." She turned to Violet. "You said I could—if you trained me. I didn't believe you then, but I do now."

"There are risks. But, yes, you can."

"Then help us!"

But Violet didn't move as Maude pushed past her to Albert and put her arm around him to ease him away from the bed. He resisted her for another second, and then he leaned against her and let her lead him back toward the exit.

Violet stood in the middle of the aisle, barring their way. "You're asking me to risk my job going against doctor's orders."

Maude scanned the room. "There's no one here to tell. The mine doctor didn't even ask his name." The nurse's eyes softened but still she hesitated. "Please, Violet! Help me save him."

"Alright." The nurse moved to the other side of Albert to help support him. "I'll give you a chance." The three began to shuffle toward the open door.

Sarah must have heard them coming. Out of the dark, her tiny frame appeared at the doorway lit by the light above the entrance. "Papa!" she called.

"Stay back!" Maude and Albert answered at the same time.

Albert turned to Maude. "Are you sure?"

"We can do this." She prayed she was right.

My Mother

BARBARA JOHNSON

Walking through this forest of my life,
my meandering feet always return to her.

Core strong, roots deep, branches stretched wide,
she welcomes me each time,
no matter how long I have been away,
and, at times, I have been
away.

For as long as I can remember,
she has been there,
a landmark,
a guidepost,
my homebase.

I sit down at her knotted feet to rest.
Soft moss and grooved bark
feeling familiar beneath my fingertips,
imprinted with childhood memories
of reaching for her grounding reassurance.

Noticing how magnificent she is today,
I think of all the seasons I have come to her,
to celebrate change in the reddening autumn,
to seek shelter in the chilling winter,
to instill hope in the burgeoning spring,
and to remind me not to wait for sunny summer days to flourish,
but to find ways to breathe life into each here and now.

A nut drops from above
and plunks me on the head.
Her leaves quiver,
perhaps from the breeze,
but more likely because she's laughing—
she loves a good joke.

And if you could see inside,
the rings would tell the story of her life,
of drought and monsoon,
of good years and bad,
of names carved inside hearts, scratched out,
then bravely carved again,
and of the haven she creates for us burrowing creatures
trying to escape the cruelty of the world.

Yet today,
all I see are the grandchildren,
swinging gleefully from her bough,
and being nourished by the fruits of her resiliency.
They delight in her,
and she in them.

She holds her place,
radiating over the forest,
as only she can.

There she is, my mother.

Beautiful, mighty.
And I will return to her,
again and again,
for as long as my feet shall wander.

One in Fifty Thousand

JANICE PHILLIPS

I TICKLED THE BACK of Ian's neck as we stood at the counter watching a teenager add tomatoes and lettuce to our subs. The three-hour drive between visiting our old friends in our hometown and returning to our new home felt long, boring, and depressing. We moved from Collingwood to Grand Bend nine months earlier for my husband's work. I missed my friends and family terribly and was sure my four kids felt the same. After almost a year of trekking back and forth, this mid-way stop was routine, a point to wipe away tears and try to shake off the sadness of missing our old life.

I rested my hands on Ian's shoulders and guided the back of his head closer to my stomach. I breathed in the little boy scent of sunscreen and dirt. His skin had darkened to a slightly golden hue and his thick hair bleached even blonder from the summer sun. As I admired my perfect little boy, I saw a mark on the back of his neck that wasn't there before…chicken pox. I foolishly breathed a sigh of relief. It was early July. He would be better soon, and the chicken pox would not impact our summer plans. The timing was perfect. Or so I thought.

Ian had just spent the weekend playing with his best friends, so I grabbed the portable phone when we got home and called to let their mom know that her boys might soon have them too. I was a little concerned since their summer was more booked than mine, but she wasn't worried. We laughed as we chatted about our kids having chicken pox and made plans to visit again in a couple weeks. This was Monday.

The next morning Ian came down to breakfast, plopped himself on the chair, head on the kitchen table, and said he wasn't hungry. His temperature was 104°F. This seemed awfully high, but I assumed the thermometer was faulty. I gave him Tylenol and took him to the couch to watch TV. The bottle of calamine lotion and cotton balls sat on the table next to him. As I dabbed pink lotion on his chicken pox, I noticed they looked funny. They weren't popping up the way they normally do. They were blackish…almost like blood blisters.

Ian, normally very rambunctious, was content to just lie on the couch watching cartoons on TV and video tapes of *The Land Before Time*. I didn't think anything was wrong. I simply chalked it up to a full weekend of play.

Wednesday morning his fever was still 102. He was restless and had even less energy. The Tylenol didn't seem to be helping. He didn't want to eat anything or drink anything. I offered chocolate puddings, ice cream, chocolate milk. Every offer was met with an incredibly polite "No, thank you!" This was NOT my son. He was perfect, yes, but this polite…never.

On Thursday morning the fever was still 102. Ian was struggling to walk.

Friday was worse. His temperature continued to hover at 102. Walking had become even more difficult. As he rested on the couch, I sat next to him and tickled his skin as I had done so many times before. He screamed. The gentlest touch was excruciatingly painful. We needed to take him to a doctor. Since our family doctor was three hours away and we didn't yet have one in the community, we drove to the nearest hospital.

Ian was in too much pain to be carried from the car, so he walked into the hospital on his toes, with his knees bent, looking like a little old man, not an active five-year-old. The admitting nurse could see that there was something very wrong, mentioning possible issues with his nervous system. She helped us get him into a room and up onto the examining table to wait for the doctor.

When the doctor came in, he stood back from the examining table and assessed my son from a distance. Not once did he touch him to witness the agony that light touch caused. Instead, his eyes dropped to my chest, and he focused more there than on my son.

I explained, "I have four kids and the older three have had chicken pox. It's never looked like this. We can't even touch him without him screaming in pain."

The doctor looked up from my breasts and told me that it was simply a mild case of the chicken pox. "I've seen much worse. You have nothing to worry about."

The nurse looked at us questioningly when we left, but I felt relieved. Doctors know what the chicken pox looks like. I was simply being overly cautious. This was my baby after all. I was being too protective, too worried.

We returned home, and I settled Ian back on the couch next to me, careful not to touch him, when all I wanted to do was cuddle him and help him feel better. I relaxed down next to him, fully trusting the doctor.

Saturday morning Ian was even worse. He slept two hours, woke screaming "Ooooww!" Slept again for a few minutes, woke in pain again, slept another hour and woke complaining his legs were burning.

I called my mother-in-law for my weekly check-in. I told her about his chicken pox. "We're giving him Tylenol but the fever's not going down. It's not getting higher, but it's not going down either. He's not eating or drinking. We can't touch him. It hurts him to walk. His chicken pox looks like blood blisters. We took him to the doctor and the doctor said it's nothing to worry about." My mother-in-law, who raised nine kids, was concerned and said, "It could be sepsis. Get another opinion."

I hung up and reluctantly called Telehealth. Who was I to question the medical expertise of the doctor? Again, I went through Ian's list of symptoms. The nurse's response was "Don't run any red lights but get him to the hospital right away. Preferably not the same hospital."

Less than an hour later we were at the emergency room in London. Ian was taken in to be examined immediately. The doctor on call could not hide the worry on her face. Seeing her look in that moment was like being punched in the stomach and having the floor ripped out from under me all at once. Why didn't I question the doctor at the other hospital and insist that I knew it was more than a mild case of the chicken pox? Why didn't I trust my instincts?

For the next few hours, doctors came in and out of Ian's room in the emergency department. Because he had chicken pox, he was quarantined in a private room. He had an infection as well. The doctors explained that it would take too long to get the test results to determine the kind of infection, and they didn't have time to wait. They started treatment immediately for a strep infection in hopes that that was what it was.

"Plastics" was consulted to determine if amputations would be required. More tests were run to see how deep the infection had gone. Ian cried that he didn't want his legs amputated. Five-year-old boys should not have to know the meaning of amputation.

That was Saturday. Five days after I had first noticed his chicken pox.

The nurses and doctors asked me how much he weighed. "Maybe fifty pounds," I said. My answer was met with questioning looks. I explained, "His sister is a year older, and she weighs fifty-five pounds. I know he weighs close to that, but a little less." I didn't understand why they were looking at me so strangely. It wasn't until I saw the pictures later that I understood. He was retaining so much fluid, he did not look like a skinny five-year-old. I'd been too close to see the gradual buildup of fluid. He looked more like he weighed eighty pounds.

Because of the fluid retention, finding a vein was difficult. For some strange reason, his one arm did not swell, and they were able to introduce drugs there. The rest of his body had ballooned in size.

When the test results came back strep was confirmed. Group A Streptococcus Necrotizing...and Chicken Pox. I sat in the hospital room stunned. I understood some of the terminology. I'd always thought of strep as a throat infection. Chicken pox was a childhood illness. And necrotizing meant flesh eating. I did not understand how the three things went together.

The doctor explained that strep can enter the body through a cut.

The weekend before, when Ian was playing with his friends, he scraped the side of his knee. It was a very small scrape that didn't even require a Band-Aid. Later they went to play in the water at the beach. It's possible the strep infection entered his body then. Because his immune system was lowered from the chicken pox, the combination made him that one child in fifty thousand who has complications from the chicken pox. Necrotizing was the result.

For the next three days I stayed by his side in his hospital room, sleeping in the chair, and attempting to lie next to him in bed when it could be managed without touching him so I wouldn't cause him more pain. Doctors and nurses came and went, asking him questions and getting polite responses, manipulating his body, drawing blood, and hearing this brave little boy object quietly when they were causing him pain with every touch.

The possibility of death was never spoken out loud, but it hung in the air and seeped into every corner of the room. Would he make it through the day? Would he make it through the night? What would I tell his sisters?

Finally, Wednesday morning, a full nine days after I noticed that first mark, the doctors came in, looked at us and said, "He's out of the woods!" He was going to live!

Thursday morning, when my husband attempted to help Ian change positions, he was still in so much pain, and my sweet, polite, perfect little boy looked up at my husband and yelled, "You fucker!" I knew the doctors were right. We really were out of the woods. Tears welled up in my eyes. I'd never been happier to hear my little boy swear.

Friday morning, as the doctor was doing her final check of Ian before he was leaving the hospital, she turned to me. "If you could do it again, would you have your children vaccinated for the chicken pox?"

I hesitated. I'm sure she expected me to respond immediately with "Yes! Absolutely!" but I was quiet. She just shook her head and turned away, obviously frustrated that reality hadn't broken through to me.

The question caught me off guard. I'd just put so much faith into the medical profession with one doctor's diagnosis and had doubted my instincts about my child's health. I needed a moment to think. Why didn't I have the kids vaccinated for the chicken pox? Where had I gotten the idea that it was risky? The only answer I could come up with was Jenny McCarthy. She was the source of so many conspiracy theories about vaccines and her voice had drowned out the scientists. Within thirty seconds my answer was "Yes! Absolutely!"—but the doctor had already left the room.

Ian's recovery lasted the entire summer. My slim five-year-old had lost so much weight that he looked skeletal when we left the hospital. Walking was still quite difficult. He continued to walk on his toes with his knees bent. Our family doctor told me, "If you don't force him to straighten his legs and use his muscles, he'll never be able to." I put his feet into the bike pedals and pushed him around the block a few times a day. I set up an exercise step in front of the TV and insisted he walk around the living room and up and down on the step during every commercial. I gave him a small desk chair on wheels so he could push himself around the house or walk around the block pushing the chair. With every cry of pain I wanted so badly to help him and to carry him, but I could not imagine him going through life unable to walk upright. He had to do this on his own.

The necrotizing part of this illness affected everywhere the chicken pox presented. Bath time that summer was spent watching dead tissue fall from the sores, leaving behind large scars…some the size of a loonie. Today, as I admire the man he has become, I'll often notice one of his scars, and in those brief moments, I vividly remember how close I came to losing him, how wonderful it was to hear my child scream profanities, and how grateful I am for the outcome and London Health Sciences Centre.

Side Gig

DOMINIQUE MILLETTE

T HE SIGN SAID THE bulk store was closing at the end of the month. Ian felt bereft as he paid for his macadamia nuts.

"I'm going to miss this place," he said to the owner, a slight man with an accent Ian couldn't place and didn't dare to query. "I hope you all land on your feet."

The man shrugged. "They say every crisis is an opportunity. You know the story of Lucky Hans? It's from the Brothers Grimm. After seven years of apprenticeship, Lucky Hans gets paid with a lump of gold the size of his head." The owner smiled wanly at the near-empty counters around him, wiping his hands with a cloth. "He gets conned into exchanging it for a horse, and thinks, 'Well, that gold was too heavy anyway. I'm a lucky man.' Then he trades the horse for a cow he can milk. The cow gets exchanged for a pig, followed by a goose, until Lucky Hans is left with a millstone which rolls away into the river. He walks away empty-handed. He's ecstatic because the millstone was too heavy. And I have to say, this store has become a millstone. I feel free. No regrets."

Ian raised his eyebrows and bowed slightly. "That's certainly a positive way to look at things. Good for you."

With the hair salon also closed, the whole centre looked deserted now. A homeless woman begged him for change, which Ian thought was hilarious, considering he might end up as her competition soon, what with the way business was going. He could see why there were fewer and fewer customers here. We're going to end up like Detroit when it went bankrupt, he thought, except with better lighting and garbage collection.

The closures were a trickle at first: the drugstore at the corner of Dundas and Richmond started the trend. Then the Starbucks went. Once the McDonald's closed down and the whole building around it emptied out like a mall in a zombie movie, the trickle turned into a flood, hitting the second-hand furniture store that had stood for twenty-five years. After that, a gift shop, two clothing retailers, the jeweller, the local tailor, and then finally, the natural food store closed in the Citi Centre. As all these businesses shut their doors, the associated relationships also disappeared, Ian thought to himself, even if it was just a hello, how are you, thank you. Those small interactions helped people feel like a part of society.

It didn't help that since the pandemic, office workers had never returned downtown in their previous numbers. Just before that, the city had torn up the main street downtown to make it festival friendly. It took months longer than planned, for two years in a row. Regular customers had a hard time navigating the chaos and went to more car-friendly stores. Finally, new corporate owners of residential buildings who wanted to maximize profits kicked hundreds of people out of their low-rent apartments. Dozens of the newly homeless ended up pushing shopping carts along the shiny new festival-friendly cobblestones and asking everyone for change, so more passersby avoided the area than ever before.

Ian slowed his pace as he exited the building, walking more gingerly. There were brown smears on the sidewalk in at least three places in front of him, maybe from a dog, but they looked human. He headed to his electronics shop in Old East Village. The letters of the Tronical Groove sign flickered in the window, and the neon palm tree next to them winked out as he came in. Sign of the times, ha ha ha, thought Ian. At least he hadn't used his name, Blezard, because if the B went out the place would look like it might be a pet shop that specialized in reptiles.

All the retailers on the street kept their doors locked so customers would have to ring the bell to get in. Jim and Irma, two local musicians who made their living with a karaoke and open mic hosting company, knocked on the window to get his attention. He suppressed a scowl. The two irritated him with a forced joviality that barely concealed their narcissistic expectation of immediate service. Still, they were company, familiar, and talented enough— and not too proud to pay their bills with work that demanded they proffer forced encouragement, copious applause and a high tolerance for off-key covers of "Sweet Caroline." He envied their easy partnership, though after his divorce he wasn't inclined to try dating again. Don't be such a pessimist, Irma would say, as she brought one woman after another into his store to browse products, to no avail.

Today, Irma needed a new laptop to run the scrolling lyrics with the big red dot that told you what word you were on. She was a singer and ran the karaoke side of the business. Jim, a bassist who also played some guitar and keyboards and sang if he had to, was the main open mic host. They could split up if they needed to get more gigs. Ian found her a Lenovo on sale, a barely used demo with a decent-sized SSD drive. Jim looked it over and added his approval.

Ian leaned over the counter. "Would you like a stand with that? Brand new, top of the line."

"No, that's all right," Irma said.

It was a delicate dance between friendly chatter and a sales pitch. Networking. Be personable. Customers need a reason to come to you instead of the competition. Ian grew to resent the need to point out, as indirectly and pleasantly as possible, that after all, they were in a store, and stores were where you bought things, especially when the rent was due and too little inventory had moved in over thirty days. The way some people looked at him rankled, as if he were emerging from lurking in dark corners, reeking of desperation, ready to drag them into an orgy of spending—or worse, to beg them unrelentingly.

What was going through their minds? That he only wanted their money? Ian wanted to shout that he needed both money and friends, but the world wouldn't let him simply smile and wave away opportunities for the sake of propriety. Too often, his exchanges with people led to awkward pauses and a poorly concealed pout of discouragement when the friend-customer left without buying anything. Jim had called him saturnine one day. Ian had had to look it up and didn't want to do it in front of Jim, so he only got offended after it was too late. Then he'd thought: Try being stuck with all this inventory and you'd be saturnine, too.

As Irma paid, Jim harrumphed.

"Have you ever thought of a side gig to bring in extra money? I mean, no offence, but there aren't a ton of people here."

Ian glanced up and answered with a twinge of annoyance in his voice. "Why? Do you have something in mind?"

Jim took a canister from his knapsack and set it on the counter. "As a matter of fact, I do. And believe me, it brings in the dough." The label read *Bernie's Protein Powder*.

It was hard for Ian not to roll his eyes. The pitch sounded like something an Amway or Tupperware salesperson would say.

"Seriously? You're hawking protein powder now?"

Jim looked offended but replied with calm confidence. "I made a few thousand last month, so seriously, yes."

Ian was impressed. Tupperware didn't usually bring in that much. Maybe Jim's suggestion wasn't such a bad idea. Just five years ago, everything had been coming up roses, the sky was the limit and all that. Tronical Groove was helping to rejuvenate the neighbourhood—not gentrifying it, just adding colour and funk and style, along with the dozen or so other new retailers moving in for the affordable rents and new-possibilities vibe. Now, the store was running one blowout sale after the other, selling at a loss half the time, with accessories the only potential profit point.

Still, Ian was skeptical. "I bet you have to pay all this inventory up front. I wouldn't have the money."

Jim shook his head. "Nope. They front you the inventory and give you hot leads, not cold ones: people who're already interested in buying. All you have to do is stash the product, call the initial sales leads, then people confirm and come in and pick it up and pay for it. You get a commission. I get my inventory from Bernie. You'd be getting it from me."

Ian felt a wave of uneasiness. "Sounds like some kind of pyramid scheme."

"It's multilevel marketing, which is not the same thing," Jim insisted. "And the product is a lot better than Amway. You wouldn't believe how easy it is to move this stuff. It isn't like those other outfits where you end up with boxes in your garage with the mice crapping all over them. Trust me."

Jim wouldn't lie about the money, Ian decided. He might be patronizing sometimes, but he was no liar. "Well, if it's working out that well for you, count me in."

For the first time in a while, he felt hope, like in that line Irma used about the feathers perching in your soul.

It was a rainy Tuesday when the bell rang in three short spurts and Ian glanced up from his wreck of an accounting folder to see a new face that looked like money. He opened the door expectantly. The well-coiffed stranger smiled with perfect teeth, just the right shade, not too bright white, and thrust out a manicured hand.

"Hello, there. I'm Bernie."

"Ian. I've heard good things!"

"They're all true. Like Jim should have explained, we front you the goods and you just have to follow up on those leads we give you and pass it on. When would you like the product?"

"As soon as you can drop it off."

"Great. I'll be giving you the list of customers when we bring you the merch."

Bernie walked out in a wave of merino wool.

The next day, he came around with two hulking guys in sweats to drop off the boxes of protein powder. He handed Ian a list of names and phone numbers. "Call these guys today. You don't want the leads to get cold."

Ian smiled. "Absolutely. I know all about that."

Bernie winked. "One business is a lot like another. Once you move this stuff, we can bring in some more."

Within a few days, the customers came in. Most of them looked like jocks, with thick necks and sweat suits, which made perfect sense. They said they were gym owners and personal trainers and swore up and down that this particular powder was magic, as hot as chia seeds or goji berries, which even Ian knew were a solid trend.

As Ian waved the last customer out of the store, his heart pounded with gratitude. The commission he'd earned in one day was as much as a week's worth of sales from the shop. He'd been right to take a chance on life, as Irma would put it.

The next drop-off was Monday. Monday came and went. No Bernie. Another week went by, with still no sign of his newest business partner. Maybe Bernie had got sick, Ian speculated. Maybe he'd been called out of town and had an accident. At least Bernie had paid him, Ian thought, and immediately felt guilty for being relieved he didn't share any of his potential misfortune. He called Jim but had to leave a message.

The bell rang insistently at opening time the next day. Police officers waved at him through the glass. One of them, the shorter of the two, was holding a paper. Ian frowned as he opened the door.

"What's up? Everything all right? Are you canvassing witnesses? Did someone get hurt?"

Given the neighbourhood, it was a logical assumption. Knife fights broke out regularly between hapless denizens of local storefront doorways struggling to keep their shoes, hats, or the little change they'd managed to beg.

The shorter officer shook his head. "No, sir. Not yet. We're here to make sure that doesn't happen. You're Mr. Blezard, the owner?"

Ian nodded, lead gathering in his chest.

The policeman waved his paper.

"We have a warrant to search the premises, including any back rooms and storage areas."

Ian started to shake, his heart thumping like a sound effect in an Edgar Allan Poe movie adaptation. He moved aside. The officers pulled out masks and gloves on the way into the storeroom. They opened every box.

The short one spoke first. "Looks like the deal we made with that Jim guy was worth it. There's enough fentanyl in here to kill half the city."

His taller colleague scoffed. "Can you believe he said he didn't know? How stupid would you have to be to think a supplement can make you that much money?"

The thump, thump, thump of Ian's heart got louder. He walked soundlessly to the door, then slipped outside with his head spinning. There was a shopping cart on his left, piled high with fragrant flotsam. He grabbed a wool toque, a scarf and a long jacket.

The owner of the shopping cart ran toward him. "Hey. Give that back!"

Ian sprinted away, trying not to gag, down the alley piled with garbage behind the store. The door to the storeroom was open. A black-capped head poked out and shouted.

"He's a runner."

They caught him easily. As they slapped the cuffs on, it occurred to Ian that he wouldn't be able to pay his lawyer with the proceeds of crime, if television procedurals were anything to go by. No phone call for him. No bail. There was no one to pay it. The store was finished.

Ian thought about the story of Lucky Hans. At least in prison there would be no rent, inventory or grocery bills.

He whistled. The melody squeezed itself out in a thin breath: *Sweet Caroline / Pah-dah pah pah.*

Still

LAURIE BROWNE

Thoughts of you hang suspended
in the air
like fine dust in sunlight.
Shaking out the flannel sheets
in your old bedroom,
I can see bits of you
everywhere.
I touch the cool plaster walls
and
trace the tiny cracks
with my fingertips.
I can almost feel the faint
pulse
of a heartbeat.
All the things you left behind
lie here
in scattered piles.
My sentimental heart—
too afraid.

The fear that I would lose
parts of you.
It took so long to finally
begin.
Should I keep this jar of foreign coins?
Could I discard this velvet ribbon,
this brooch in the shape of a songbird,
this random spool
of thread?
All of these things
sit quietly
awaiting my judgment.
I swear that I heard
your last breath,
as the nurse's shoes squeaked
toward me.
Now, I am here
in this house that you
made home.

I gaze out of the window
that faces north
and
spot a cardinal
in the cherry tree.
Its scarlet crown
bobs in and out of the clouds
of pink blooms.
You are *still* here.
Strands of you,
strong as spider's silk
sway in the corners
of this old house.

My other half hisses in my ear:
"It's just a draft."
I nod my head
in feigned agreement,
all the while
knowing.

All Trees Matter

GEORGE ALLAN TUCKER

I N 1970, AINSLEY Oakley and his wife Juniper purchased ten acres—severed from the five-hundred-acre Scott MacDaniels pioneer farm—that backed onto the south branch of the Thames River. Maurice Hay, a local building contractor, designed and built a 1,200-square foot, three-bedroom pine log home on a convenient one-acre hilltop site, chosen for its panoramic view overlooking the Thames. The remaining acreage supported an old-growth forest that spread down to the riverbank. Ainsley was employed at the Canadian National Railway car shops on Egerton Street, while Juniper worked at Ealing Pharmacy on Hamilton Road East. Over the next few years, three children were born—Michael, Gordon and Edythe.

Their property was forested with quite a variety of native trees: primarily Manitoba maples and white pine, with a scattering of birch, beech, pin oak and black spruce. Some of these life-giving trees dated back over five hundred years. A lone eastern white cedar, estimated to be over a thousand years old, towered over the tops of all the other trees.

These forested areas supported a wide variety of wildlife—especially birds! Over the years, Ainsley became an avid bird-watcher, and together with his birder friends he identified close to a hundred different species along the riverbank and in the surrounding woodlands. His favourite "king of the woods" was a pileated woodpecker he named Pecker Head. The family also enjoyed the company of Frisky, a white-tailed deer, as well as Wiley Coyote and a local red fox and family.

They set up a sugar shack and collected sap to produce Oakley Maple Syrup each spring, and harvested honey from beehives set up near Juniper's garden. All in all, as they used to tell their relatives back in Scotland, they lived in "Nature's Canadian Paradise"!

Everything changed early one Monday morning in April.

It had been fifty years since they moved into Nature's Canadian Paradise. Their kids had all grown up and moved out into the local community.

Most mornings, they would be awakened by familiar melodious bird songs, but not this morning. The *vroom, vroom, brrr* of chainsaws echoed through the trees and into their bedroom. Rocky, their black Lab, started barking and Mojo, their cat, scurried under the bed.

Ainsley was, to say the least, shocked at what he was hearing. He immediately got up, dressed and left the house. He walked west through his woodlot to investigate the annoying sound coming from deep inside MacDaniels Woods. When he reached the old split-rail fence that separated his property from Scott's, the noise intensified. He climbed over and carefully picked his way through the underbrush toward the *vroom* noises.

Within a few minutes, he encountered a team of men in safety vests and helmets, chainsaws in hand. An ancient red maple lay on the ground at their feet. Numerous other tree trunks had large "X" signs painted in red on them, obviously waiting for a similar fate. Upon questioning the apparent team leader, identified by the traditional white supervisor's helmet he was wearing, Ainsley learned that a London developer—Gorelands—had recently purchased the MacDaniels Farm along with most of the properties east, west and south along the south side of the Thames. Apparently, a two-hundred-home luxury housing development had recently been approved by London's City Council.

Needless to say, the thought of any housing project being built near Ainsley's nature paradise caused him to deliver a plethora of polite objections, finishing off with a promise to organize a campaign against the whole project. As he stormed away from his unexpected meeting, the *vroom, vroom, brrr* of the chainsaws could be heard in the background.

He wondered, as he hurried back home, why he had not been informed by City Hall of such a major development project.

Arriving back home, he explained to Juniper his encounter with the chainsaw team, ending with the words, "We'll have to find a way to stop the entire project before it destroys Nature's Canadian Paradise!"

He called his boss Maurice at the CNR shops to explain that he wasn't feeling well and would not be coming into work that week. Juniper, likewise, called her boss Irene at the pharmacy to explain she had to stay home for a few days to care for her husband who had come down with chills and a high fever—"likely the flu," she lied.

The couple then sat at their kitchen table to develop a plan of action to prevent the destruction of these precious old-growth woodlands that provided a haven for a wide variety of birds and wildlife, not to mention the trees' collective contribution to the very air that they breathed.

A phone call to City Hall to challenge the approval of such a devastating housing project went to voicemail hell and left Ainsley hanging on hold. Talk about frustration!

His next call was to the president of Bird Friendly London to report on the development project's objective and his concern for the local bird population, especially since it was their nesting season.

He then left a message for Willy Wyatt, his local representative for Nature Canada. Willy's government organization had just released Canada's *2030 Nature Strategy and Accountability Bill.* Willy was equally upset at the news!

During the week that followed, alarm bells began ringing all along the Thames. Ainsley spent hours reaching out to the local media, MPPs and MPs of all stripes, and key contacts in adjoining southern municipalities like Glencoe and Ridgetown. Although everyone was very supportive of Ainsley's concerns for Mother Nature, the consensus was that most likely it was too late to stop the development—the horses had left the stable.

According to one local journalist who monitored City Hall matters for *The London Free Press*, the development project was shoved through Council in February with a 7–3 vote in favour, apparently influenced by the size of the project, the creation of good-paying jobs and the projected property tax revenues. No mention of the fact that the mayor's brother-in-law owned Gorelands Property Development LLC, the project developer!

By this point, Ainsley had already decided he would have to take personal and drastic action to draw attention to what he considered a travesty against nature. He went about organizing Bird Friendly London members who were willing to take part in a blockade of the entrance being used to access the site. Representatives of the Thames River Conservation Authority were invited to take part as well but declined the invitation on the grounds of a potential conflict of interest. So much for their "authority."

Moving down his list, he contacted the Thames River Anglers Association, where he got a welcoming reception and an offer to solicit volunteer support from their membership to take part in the blockade.

Following the positive response from the TRAA, he reached out to the Director of Public Works for the Municipality of Thames Centre and the Thames-Sydenham and Region Source Protection Committee, both of which were responsible under the *Clean Water*

Act. (The *CWA* is intended to ensure the protection of municipal drinking water sources—including rivers, lakes and groundwater—and subsequently human health and the environment.)

Unfortunately, the Director of Public Works, Joe Bredner, could not commit to such participation and admitted that he was not fully unaware of the development. He did agree to look into the matter, but in his words, "the opposing players [had] already forfeited the game."

Ainsley was an increasingly unhappy camper. His position was that there was plenty of open land throughout the area that would be better suited to housing developments. Destroying one of the few remaining regional natural habitats, especially one that is adjacent to a major river, was simply unacceptable. Coincidentally, a disastrous spring-runoff scenario affecting a First Nations community's water supply had recently been in the news. Warning bells should have been ringing loud and clear during Council's review of the proposed development.

Nevertheless, Ainsley felt it was important to take prompt action to at least stop the project before too much damage could be inflicted. His coordinated defensive blockade plan was set to begin the following week.

At the appointed hour early Monday morning, volunteer protesters assembled outside the gate of the Gorelands development. Ainsley addressed the group, which numbered about fifty individuals, including family members, neighbours, friends, and members of the TRAA. David Harris and Kathy Ayers, two of the dissenting City Councillors, as well as a few hikers, rounded out the group. Ainsley thanked them for coming out and for raising their concerns considering the damage about to be inflicted on the pristine Thames River Valley forest in their community.

He explained that his property was adjacent to the development project and, since he felt his family would be most greatly affected, he would be taking the first step in confronting the development—by chaining himself and wife Juniper to the entrance gate! He produced a long piece of chain and a padlock. He ran the chain through the gate fencing and around the gate post, then around their waists, and secured the padlock. There was an immediate round of cheers and applause.

Some of the protesters had brought folding chairs with them, and others simply stood by listening to the words from the two dissenting Councillors. They encouraged the group to stand firm.

At this point, a Jeep pulled up and parked at the side of the road. It was Billy Richardson, President of the TRAA. He approached Ainsley and Juniper, thanking them for their courage in trying to stop the development. He added his concerns, saying that previous construction projects close to the Thames further downstream had already caused a noticeable decline in the pickerel run.

At 8:30 a.m., a Crump Stump Services truck pulled up in front of the gate, accompanied by the same crew Ainsley had encountered in the woods previously. The owner and supervisor, Josh Crump, approached Ainsley and Juniper and politely asked them to remove the chain that anchored them to the gate and leave the property immediately.

The old couple sat staring into the woods in silence.

Mr. Crump asked them again to "*please* move." No response.

The crowd booed the Crump team.

It was a standoff!

Crump and his team packed up and left.

By five o'clock, the crowd of protesters started to disperse, eventually leaving Ainsley, Juniper and their children and grandchildren alone at the gate.

Ainsley had brought along a folding camp cot and sleeping bag, explaining to Juniper that he intended to stay chained to the gate overnight in order to confront Crump's Team again the next morning—assuming they would be making a return visit to the job site.

Although she wasn't happy with his decision, Juniper released herself from the chain and reluctantly headed back home. Their son Michael, who lived with his family in a nearby Hamilton Road townhouse, tried to convince his dad to go home and come back in the morning to continue his protest, but Ainsley—who now described himself as an Olde Tree—refused to leave. Michael returned later that evening to spend the night with his dad.

After sunrise the next morning, Juniper showed up with a thermos of hot coffee, a couple of boiled eggs and her own folding camp chair. Michael had to leave for work, leaving the Olde Couple alone at the gate.

Over the next half hour, Billy from the TRAA showed up to continue his support, along with a few of the neighbours who were present on Monday. Dissenting Councillor Kathy Ayers arrived next, having ridden her bicycle all the way from her home on Highbury Avenue.

The scene was now set!

Shortly thereafter, Josh Crump and the Crump Stump Services Team showed up, along with Karen Graham, a representative from Gorelands, the developer.

Ms. Graham approached the Olde Couple and proceeded to explain the company's position. They had been granted approval by City Council for the housing development on the land they now owned and had every right to proceed with the project. She tried to assure Ainsley that they would be clearing away only those trees that would be in the way of the actual home sites or would interfere with the building of connecting roadways into the subdivision. She also gave a verbal promise that their ongoing plan was to plant many replacement trees once the development was up and running.

Ainsley countered by challenging Ms. Graham's story based on the fact that a large number of trees within one hundred metres of the Thames riverbank and throughout the entire forested area had already been marked for removal with that fateful red X painted onto their trunks.

At that point, Karen Graham raised the question with Josh Crump. Josh's response was, to say the least, unexpected. He disagreed with the information provided by Ms. Graham, saying that their contract was to basically clear-cut the development area to make it easier to construct the roadways into the area in advance of starting to install the underground services, put in foundations, and erect the houses. He added that the planting of replacement trees would only take place after all the roads and homes were finished and in place.

More booing followed from the protesters.

Ms. Graham was noticeably upset and immediately left the site. Josh and his team followed. It was then that Ainsley noticed a police car parked a short distance up the road. He assumed that they would have intervened should any violence have erupted at the gate.

In light of the obvious disagreement between Gorelands and his contractor, Ainsley unlocked himself from the gate. Congratulating his fellow protesters for their support, he packed up and went home.

The next day, Kathy Ayers called for an emergency meeting of City Council to reveal a problem with respect to the approved Gorelands plans. The idea of a clear-cut of the lands had not been included in the plans as presented to Council. During the debate that followed, the mayor's possible conflict of interest in promoting the plan, based on his relationship with the owner of Gorelands, was vigorously challenged by the original two dissenting Councillors. As a result, the Council voted to suspend their previous approval pending a clarification from Gorelands.

Arguments were presented with respect to the idea of clear-cutting old-growth forests, citing the ongoing efforts by local Indigenous communities to preserve woodlands.

Before the Council meeting adjourned, Kathy Ayers asked her fellow Councillors to send a letter of appreciation to Ainsley and his family for their courage and persistence in bringing the situation to light.

A few days later the official letter from City Council arrived in the mail. The one thing still missing in Council's letter was a guarantee that the practice of allowing developers to strip the land of all trees would be unacceptable in future, and that City approval would be required for any trees to be removed.

"We're not out of the woods yet!" Ainsley said.

Coated

C.J. FREDERICK

London, Ontario, 1974

THE FAMILY DOG'S alarmed barking was her cue to jump into action. For weeks, each time Mocha woofed, Ella performed her ritual of tiptoeing onto the front step, reaching into the mailbox, and fishing around for a letter-sized envelope stashed among the flyers. She was waiting for the letter that would determine her next direction.

It arrived on a Monday.

Ella ripped open the envelope from Western. She paused as her eyes scanned the paper, then she shrieked, leaving her mother to guess if it was from delight or disappointment. She displayed most emotions as soon as she felt them, certainly a trait inherited from her father's Italian side of the family.

"Well, don't just stand there." Marta's eyes welled with tears as she stared at her daughter's shaking hands, still grasping the fluttering paper. "Spill it!" Ella didn't mean to prolong her mother's agony while waiting for an explanation, but she found herself at an unusual loss for words.

The words flooded out in a flurry. "It's a YES! I'm in!" Another shriek filled the foyer, alerting neighbours and possibly birds in the trees above that Western had agreed to admit her in September. The studying, the steadfastness, the sacrifices. All of it had led to this moment when the future arrived in an envelope. And if everything progressed as hoped, the family would boast its first university graduate and a future lawyer.

"Oh, Ella. You did it. I'm so proud." In her mother's tight embrace, Ella experienced the excitement rippling beneath her skin like an electrical current. Coming from a large family meant Marta's own dreams of getting an advanced education were never realized. By sixteen, she'd been working at the shoe factory sewing leather pieces for fifty cents an hour. "So proud of you," she whispered into her daughter's chestnut hair.

Ella broke her mother's embrace and jumped into the air.

"I've gotta go tell Dad."

The telephone factory, one of the Forest City's largest employers, was a few blocks west, and if she pedalled with the tailwind, she'd be able to catch her father on one of his afternoon breaks to share her news. It was a noisy, dirty environment, but Stefano was proud of his high-paying factory job. He had arrived in Canada from war-torn Italy in the late 1940s as a young adult and didn't have much education, but he landed a job at Northern Electric when he was seventeen and it had provided his family with a small home and a comfortable life. Ella folded the acceptance letter, jammed it into her jeans pocket and scrambled for the door.

Marta dashed to the closet and dug out her daughter's pink K-Way zip-up that she had given to her at her last birthday, placing it on her shoulders as Ella slipped past her. "Don't forget your coat."

1984

She gulped the last drop of vodka from the dusty bottle, then ripped at her cuticles until a drip of blood seeped from her nail bed. *Shit, that hurts*. But the momentary physical pain dulled the turmoil rattling in her head. She had a few hours to gather the essentials to bring to the women's shelter. The social worker at the ER had arranged Ella a spot after seeing her blackened eye and grip marks around her throat and then learning that Ella didn't have any family to turn to. *The most dangerous time in the cycle of domestic abuse is when the one being abused is trying to leave the relationship.* The words echoed off the peeling walls of the smoke-stained apartment. *I always hated that peach colour*, she thought. Ella struggled to retrieve her suitcase from the closet and began throwing pants and sweaters into it without inspecting or folding them.

She pulled at the Western sticker peeling off the side of the suitcase. The last time she'd used it was her political science field trip to Ottawa, where they sat in the House of Commons gallery and watched the debates.

Guess I fucked that up.

Ella's university days seemed so far behind her. Not finishing had been her deepest regret, even worse perhaps than her hookup with the new guy who joined the evening shift at the factory where she had started working to earn a bit of extra money for school. "He's below you," her mother had warned. "And he distracts you from your studies." But her mother's gentle guidance, the pillar she relied upon for advice, disappeared when Marta died. First her mother was diagnosed with an aggressive cancer, and then her father passed away from a heart attack. Ever since the loss of both parents during her third year in university, she had been floating untethered. That's when she had picked up her first bottle and discovered that the contents numbed her.

CLOMP.

CLOMP.

CLOMP.

CLOMP.

The steel toe of his work boots smacked on the risers in the stairwell. Their apartment had thin walls, and they could hear every conversation that took place in the hall, each arrival or departure from the building. They had rented the modest one-bedroom apartment in a three-storey walk-up when they first got together six years ago. The previous occupants had left behind stained floral curtains and a broken laundry hamper, both items they still used.

CLOMP.

CLOMP.

He's home way early. The vodka had dulled Ella's reactions. He slammed his foot on each step. *He must've caught a ride with Tom. Shit!*

Ella zipped the case shut and dragged it to the living room. She might still have a chance to push past him if she hurried. A taxi was waiting at the curb. She just had to make it down the stairs.

Too late.

He filled the doorway and surveyed the living room in front of him. His eyes targeted her battered suitcase. "Just where the hell do you think you're going?" The air disappeared from the room. The only sound was the humming and sputtering of the fridge.

Trapped.

Ella felt herself shrinking behind the suitcase. Her escape route was blocked. *Shit.*

"I, uh…"

"Just say it." Steam rose from his forehead as his face turned crimson.

She focused on the wall, not daring to look at him. "I'm done. I can't do this anymore."

The ten seconds of silence stretched like an elastic band. She waited for the snap. With him, there was always a snap.

Nothing.

He did not respond. (*Was he letting her go?* She wasn't sure.)

She grasped the suitcase's handle. (*Could it be this easy?* She wasn't sure.)

Ella felt the last swig of vodka reappearing at the back of her throat, burning as it swirled; it gave her the courage she needed to make her move. She pulled the suitcase toward the door, snagging it on the doormat.

He moved aside to give her space.

"If you walk through that door, don't ever come back."

Ella squeezed herself and the suitcase through the space between him and the doorframe. His body heat seared her as she passed. Ella kept her gaze forward. *Almost free.*

SNAP.

The elastic band had snapped, just like it always did. His fingers burned into her flesh as he pinched her shoulder and crunched her trapezius muscle, causing her to wince. "You stupid piece of shit," he said.

The man who lived across the hall opened his door on his way to the garbage chute. "Everything okay?" Mr. Silva had arrived in Canada from the Azores after the war. He was the building's first tenant and monitored the comings and goings of all its residents. Ella enjoyed the brief conversations she shared with him at the mailbox. He reminded her of her father. The old man shuffled down the hall, trash bag tucked under his arm, waving at Ella to follow him. "Come, come."

He released his grip on her shoulder. Ella summoned her remaining courage, broke free, and scurried down the hallway, dragging the suitcase behind her, shoulder still burning. The bruise would emerge by tomorrow, but for now, each step delivered her closer to a new start.

Following Mr. Silva's steady path, she turned back to see if he had followed. He was not there. The stairwell was within sight. *Just keep moving.* Her eyes focused on the orange carpet, stained with god knows what. *I sure won't miss this dump.*

"Hey!" His husky roar filled the hallway.

Ella cowered against the wall. *Shit.* He tossed the object toward her. It landed in a flattened heap near the garbage disposal door. The pink K-Way, the one her mother had given her a decade before, was now freshly shredded almost in half. The gash in the fabric looked like a fault line on the Earth following a quake. He knew it was a gift from her late mother.

"Take your fucking coat!"

1994

Bridget swallowed the last sip of her now-cold coffee from the soggy paper cup. An hour earlier, it had been a searing beverage to jump-start her morning shift. This was her tenth year with the London Police Force. One of the first female constables, and now a detective, she had ascended the ranks, maybe not as quickly as some of her male counterparts, but she was still rising. Long ago, she discovered that, in her job, each day introduced a new cast of characters and scenes. *Who will I meet today?* As she sat at a traffic light, the static call came over her radio.

"Incident on Jalna with two 10-45s. Officers at the scene, detectives dispatched."

Two victims, both deceased. Despite her hardened outlook, the protective shell that all cops eventually develop after interacting with people on their worst days, it sent a shiver. London wasn't a particularly violent city, at least by American standards, but this was a potential murder scene.

Her cruiser pulled up behind two other cars, each with their lights flashing, broadcasting an unwelcome wakeup call across the sleepy street. She slammed the shifter into Park, turned off the ignition and marched up the cement walkway, taking care to avoid the split pavers that threatened to trip her and swallow her boot. She presented her badge to the officer standing at the entrance as he nodded. "Is Bob here?" she asked him. He pointed her through the doorway. "Up the stairs, second floor, first apartment on the right."

She already knew that the police had visited this apartment multiple times, sometimes called by neighbours, sometimes called by the female occupant. Bridget jogged up the stairs two at a time.

CLOMP.

CLOMP.

CLOMP.

CLOMP.

The impact of her polished boots hitting the cement steps echoed in the stairwell.

CLOMP.

CLOMP.

"Bridge, over here." Bob waved her in. He was standing beside a man's body, splayed on his back and missing half his skull. The crater shape seemed like an exit wound. The gun resting beside him, also a clue. Bridget breathed in; the gunpowder scent still lingered in the apartment's stale air. "GSW, seems self-inflicted. Neighbours called after hearing gunshots. They said they heard door-slamming and arguing around three and then gunshots around six." He pointed at the framed photo on the wall, where the slogan *OUR STORY* twinkled in gold lettering, a burly man with his arms wrapped around a laughing woman posing at the Port Stanley pier on the shore of nearby Lake Erie. "That's him. And the female, she's in the bedroom. Here, let me show you."

Bridget braced herself. Her previous years of work as a constable had forced her to confront the tangled world of domestic disputes, her least favourite call, the ones she (and most officers she knew) dreaded. Most were dealt with by first separating the two parties, then listening to both sides, and finally carting one away for the cooldown period. But some domestics were bombs with fuses already lit. And the problem with bombs? You didn't know the length of the fuse or when it had been lit.

She followed Bob into the cramped bedroom, almost tripping on a half-opened suitcase on the floor next to the bed. She noted the worn-out sticker half-peeled, the iconic purple mustang threatening to stampede out of the room. Bridget stared at the woman, whose brown eyes bulged from her reddened face, bruising around her throat. Bridget scanned the room. The nightstand hosted an assortment of nearly empty liquor bottles, lined up like a queue at the theatre except for the one that was knocked over and had spilled its contents onto the surface. "So, they argued, he strangled her, then he did himself in. But let's see what the evidence shows."

Bob nodded. "Yup. Killing someone with your bare hands, a crime of passion."

Bridget took out her notepad and scribbled some cursory observations of the scene.

One-bedroom apartment, scruffy and cluttered.

Alcohol present.

Signs of a struggle.

Signs of someone leaving or returning.

One victim.

One perpetrator.

She mapped her next steps in her mind. IDing the victims, working with forensics, and interviewing potential witnesses. A full day that would stretch into night, with a new cast and new scenes, but the same tired story.

Man and woman fight.

Woman tries to leave.

Man kills woman.

The most dangerous time in the cycle of domestic abuse is when the one being abused is trying to leave the relationship. She recalled the phrase from the women's shelter brochure. The case manager had handed it to her on the night that she checked herself in. Her secret, her shame, but her key to understanding the distressed women she met across the city. Bridget had both witnessed and experienced this pattern. To the casual observer, the solution seemed obvious: Just leave.

L-E-A-V-E.

But Bridget knew that to the battered woman, leaving often set in motion a repetitive cycle of returning to the relationship later, disarmed by the rosy promises of "It'll be different this time" and the hollow pleas of "Just gimme another chance." She once read that the average woman left her partner seven times before leaving for good. *And sometimes*, she thought as she looked at the woman's lifeless form draped across the messy bed, *she returns one too many times*.

Bridget sighed. It had taken her three attempts before she broke free from her own relationship.

Bob interrupted the planning unfolding in her mind. "Ya know, I'll never understand why they stay." She followed Bob back into the living room. Of course he didn't understand; few did. "Damn, these rental buildings keep their heat turned up like a sauna." Bob wiped his brow, transferring a glistening layer of sweat from his forehead to his palm.

"Don't sweat on the evidence, Bob." Her sardonic comment landed in the middle of the room.

Silence, except for the humming of the ancient fridge in the kitchen.

A smile crept across Bob's face, and he punched her shoulder. "We're gonna be here a while, Bridge. C'mon. I'll take your coat."

Doctor Transmogrify

ADAM LOVE

Kansas City, Missouri, 2104

TOMMY GAZED OUT the window of an abandoned robotics factory at the edge of the city. He squinted as he flicked his shock of stiff brown hair away from his freckled face. Beside him a shiny white roboPet three feet in height spun around on two fat wheels, its catlike eyes blinking as it watched the boy.

"Look Dad!" Tommy shouted, pointing up. "A cloudSkimmer! It's flying really low! What kind is it, Bobo?"

The roboPet focused its over-large camera eyes on the object. "That's a Class-5 Dreadnaught, Tommy! Very spiffy," it said in a cheerful voice like a chipmunk on helium.

Tommy's father Nicolai walked over the cluttered factory floor, following Tommy's voice in the distance, dodging assembly line parts and manufacturing robots covered in dust. He was a tall, thin man with close-cropped curly hair and round blue-tinted glasses as thick as bottle caps. In one hand he held a vidScreen, reading a message on it from his wife Aurora. She had died a few months before from a pulse rifle blast while they were fleeing a Skyway invasion force. He read the message for the hundredth time.

My dear Nicolai: Bobo is my last gift to you and Tommy. I'm sorry his arm is broken. Take him to Doctor Transmogrify. For Tommy he's a companion. For you, a difficult choice. Do the right thing, Nicolai. End this madness. At the bottom was a set of geo-coordinates. The message puzzled him. What difficult choice? Who was Doctor Transmogrify?

"What did you say, son?" Nicolai said, arriving at the window. He looked up and his face went white. A massive hybrid dirigible with large drone-like propellers was approaching at top speed. "That's a military craft! Get away from the window! Now!" He grabbed the boy's hand and ducked under an assembly platform. The building shook as a bomb exploded nearby.

"That was close," Tommy said.

Once, many years ago, they'd had a happy, comfortable life. But then the wars came, endless wars fought by large AI robot armies financed by the super-rich. And by now, no one really knew who was fighting who or for what reason.

They heard the sound of more explosions in the distance. "Tommy, we have to get out of here," Nicolai said. "This whole area is a war zone. We're still on a mission, remember?"

"To follow Mom's coordinates and find Doctor Transmogrify, right Dad? And then fix Bobo's arm!"

"Yes, Tommy. Let's move out, soldiers!"

"Yes sir, Dad sir! Move out, Bobo!"

The roboPet took the lead, saying, "Hup, one, hup, two…" while Tommy marched behind him.

They left the factory and passed through a market district with abandoned buildings on all sides, scavenging for food and supplies. As they emerged from one of the small shops, a giant mech walker appeared around a corner, firing upon them with its shoulder guns. Pulse bolts exploded on the ground in front of them.

"Take cover, Tommy! In there!" He pointed to a shop across the road with an orange brick facade that said Noodle Goddess above the ornate double-door entrance. They both ran and lunged inside, the roboPet trailing behind.

"Hurry, Bobo!" Tommy yelled, but one of the strafing bolts hit the bot directly as it rolled through the doorway. Bobo flew inside like a rocket, narrowly missing Tommy's head, and crashed into a counter at the back of the room.

They both looked at each other for a moment.

"They missed us again, Dad! But what about Bobo?" The boy retrieved the roboPet and sat him down on the floor. "Talk to me, Bobo!" But Bobo's lights were out and he didn't move. Tears came to Tommy's eyes.

"Bobo's dead, Dad! He can't die, can he?"

His dad patted the boy on the shoulder. "He took a hard hit, Tommy. Let me see what I can do."

Nicolai feared the worst as he reset the bot and turned it on. But to his surprise, Bobo's eyes lit up and made chiming noises as it went through the boot-up process.

"He's alive!" Tommy shouted, wiping his eyes.

The robot moved its arms and wheeled in a circle. Its left arm flailed helplessly. When it tried to bend at the waist there was a grinding motor sound.

"There's a big dent on his right side," Tommy said with a worried look. "And his power is at two percent."

"His power pack must have been damaged. He's lucky to be in one piece," Nicolai said. "Bobo's built a lot stronger than I thought. That was a pulse blast that hit him. This is no ordinary robot, Tommy. His outer shell must be made of nanofiber… it's odd."

"But Dad, he's like an old man now. He can barely move anything. Poor Bobo! We need to get him to Dr. Transmogrify."

Nicolai frowned. "We can only hope that Doctor Transmogrify has replacement parts. But none of that matters if we don't replace his power pack. At two percent, he's got 1.2 hours left, according to his power readout here. If his core is without power for more than fifteen minutes, he will lose all of his memory. And then…"

Tommy put his hand on the roboPet's dented body. "Then Bobo will be dead forever. He won't be my Bobo anymore."

"Don't worry, Tommy, we'll find a way to save him." But in his heart, he knew the chances were slim. It was a unique model and very intricate in design. Nicolai was a robotics expert and knew more than almost anyone on the planet about robot design, having worked in the field of robotics fabrication for many years before the robot wars uprooted everyone.

"Well, the good news is we're really close now," he continued. "Bobo, how close are we to the coordinates for Doctor Transmogrify?"

"Forty miles north of here, Nicolai." The bot's voice was different now, metallic and deep, like a soldierBot's. Nicolai was puzzled by it.

"What is the fastest way to get there?" Nicolai asked.

"What is your time frame?" Bobo asked.

"When your power pack dies."

"Then your only option is the autoRail. According to my most recent data, there is an underground autoRail which passes by there and is still in good repair."

"How old is your most recent data?"

"Ten years, four months and seventeen days."

Nicolai shook his head. He knew the gridNet communication network was destroyed years ago.

"Well, we'll just have to take our chances on the autoRail. Bobo, are there any entrances nearby?" Nicolai asked.

"The autoRail is a top-secret military project. All the access points are classified. Nicolai, as Chief Robotics Engineer at Aeon Corporation and highest-ranking military commander in this region, you have clearance for Level 3 military intelligence. Would you like to be granted access?"

Nicolai could not believe what he was hearing. "But I no longer…that was a long time…how is this even?…yes, yes I would."

"*Access granted.* The closest entry is at Hyperion Labs. I can take you there."

"Wait, hold on—military commander? What does that mean?"

"It means you have full command of the personnel, facilities and rocket launching bases in this—"

"Whoa whoa, your information must be a decade out of date, I'm not a general, I—"

"Dad, what's going on?" Tommy interrupted. "He doesn't sound like Bobo anymore!"

"I know, Tommy. Now he's like a super elite tactical assist bot. I don't understand how an ordinary domestic roboPet would have this other ability. The microchip for it costs a fortune and they're as rare as a kiwi bird. It must have switched modes when it got that dent."

"But I want *my* Bobo—"

"I know, Tommy. Maybe super elite Bobo can help us to get ordinary Bobo back. Show us the way, Bobo!"

Tommy and his father started moving toward the back door of the noodle shop. But the roboPet stopped short, scanning the door.

"Not that way," Bobo announced. "My sensors indicate three armed turboBots approaching from the back alley. The front door is now clear. We should go that way."

They went out and moved through the city, taking cover in various buildings and picking a path through the maze-like wreckage. The roboPet could still move quickly on its wheels and always managed to find a clear path. In several minutes Bobo had led them to an unmarked metal door in a long concrete wall. Bobo made a series of clicks and whistles. The door slid open, revealing a well-lit stairwell to the autoRail.

Forty-seven minutes had passed by the time they arrived at the correct station. By then, Bobo's power was at zero percent and Tommy was panicking.

"Let's go Dad! C'mon, hurry."

Nicolai carrying Bobo, they sped up the stairs, through a long hallway and into the centre of a spacious, tiled room. A hologram appeared of a smartly dressed woman in business attire. She blinked a few times.

"Hello, Nicolai. Where can I direct you?"

"We have a domestic T74 roboPet which will expire in…"—Nicolai checked Bobo's back view panel—"under three minutes. Is there anything you can do to save it?"

There was no response. But in a few moments, three repairBots came zooming down the left hallway toward them.

They stopped in front of Nicolai. Two of the bots gently clutched Bobo's body while the third removed Bobo's power pack and inserted two wires connected to an external power bank.

Bobo's lights lit up.

"He's alive again! You did it!" Tommy was jumping up and down with joy.

A balding man with grey hair and a long-tailed white coat came down the hall and walked up to Nicolai.

"Hello friends!" he said expansively. "Such a surprise to see human faces after so many months. Nicolai, a great honour to meet you. Your credentials are impeccable! I'm Jules Aleppo—"

"But we need to find Doctor Transmogrify, sir," said Tommy.

"Ah. Ah yes. Many years ago, I had a repair shop by that name. You may call me Doctor Transmogrify if it suits you, young man. And Tommy, what a special roboPet you have there."

"Thanks Doctor! But he's still a mess. Can you fix him? Can you make him just like he was?"

"Certainly, my boy! Let's take him to the lab and see what we have here."

He motioned them down the hall and into a vast high-tech factory with a host of mechanized workstations. There were bots in various stages of repair—gigantic mechWalkers with arms being reattached, turboBots in pieces on benches, and many older-model soldierBots.

The doctor took them to a raised metal platform surrounded by mechanical arms with claw, wrench and laser attachments, and the repairBots placed Bobo upon it.

"You said this little roboPet was special," Nicolai said. "What makes it so special?"

"Indeed, indeed…let me explain to you the unique history of the T74 roboPet. You see, only a few hundred of these were ever made, at the GenTech Facility in Houston, RioStar region. I've read your file, Nicolai—you were chief engineer there, yes?"

Nicolai nodded, a faraway look in his eyes.

"The GenTech engineers had created a bot so advanced that it could clone itself, powered by the Akumu-13 chip, a technological marvel, the greatest achievement in the field of robotics. Before GenTech was destroyed by the Pacific Axis, a group of engineers sought to hide the few remaining chips to preserve this rare and valuable technology. So, they implanted them in a few domestic bots. But all of them were lost in the following years. Except yours. And now by some miracle, you brought it here!"

As he spoke, a mechanical arm removed Bobo's breast plate. Inside a small compartment were six tiny, rectangular silicon wafers. The doctor carefully removed them and laid them out in his hand.

"The Akumu-13! I thought they were all destroyed!" Nicolai said with a look of awe and wonder. "I created the code for those chips. It was my life's work. So beautiful!"

"You may not believe it, but right now, at this moment, these six chips are worth more than all the gold in the world!"

Nicolai looked up. "How so? They're a miracle of engineering, no doubt. But I fail to understand why they're so valuable."

The doctor smiled. "Don't you see? The Pacific Axis, the Fusion Alliance, Skyway—all the armies of the world are running out of robots. Most of the factories have been destroyed. They have no chips left! Here in this facility, we have four intact Akumu-level turboBots, but no chips for them. With these chips here in my hand we can now replicate more chips, and at great speed! In a matter of a few months the Fusion Alliance will have tens of thousands of Akumu turboBots, which are much more advanced in military capability than even the best turboBots. We can change the course of the wars! We will sweep across the continent, crushing all robot armies before us."

Hearing this speech, Nicolai was silent.

Tommy spoke up. "But can you fix my Bobo? I don't care about all that other stuff. Please, doctor, can you?"

The doctor looked with compassion at Tommy. "Of course, it will only take a few minutes, we have all the parts here. It's the least we can do for you, poor boy!"

And true to his word, Bobo's arm was replaced, his programming circuits were restored and a new side plate was installed. A repairBot set him on the ground.

"Bobo?" Tommy said. "Is it you?"

"Hello Tommy!" Bobo replied cheerfully in his high-pitched voice. "I feel fantastic." He spun around on his fat wheels.

"That's my Bobo! He's okay, Dad! I can't believe it."

Nicolai patted him on the back. "Mission accomplished, Tommy. Thank you, Doctor, uh, Mr. Aleppo."

"My pleasure, Nicolai. Your gift will change everything! I must be on my way home for the day. Happy travels, wherever you're going."

The doctor waved as the trio walked out of the building and straight down the first road they could find. It was a beautiful summer day and the sun was high in the sky. Nicolai had no destination in mind. It was enough to be travelling anywhere with his son, who was as happy as could be, chatting with his favourite roboPet companion.

After a few hours on the road, Nicolai stopped and read his wife's message again. "I understand now. *A difficult choice.*" He hesitated, looked back with deep sadness and regret, then kneeled next to Bobo and whispered a set of instructions.

In two minutes, he heard a whistling noise behind him and turned around. He could still see the factory, a tiny dot in the distance. The whistling came from a rocket making a downward arc in the sky. There was a booming sound as it made a direct hit on the factory.

"What was that, Dad?" Tommy said, looking back.

Nicolai patted him on the head. "Nothing, Tommy. Just another rocket."

But to himself he thought: *My life's work, my great dream, in those last six pieces of silicon—created to serve humanity, only to be weaponized for endless war—gone now, forever. The madness has ended. Thank you, Aurora.* And he wiped tears from his eyes.

Away

ELEANOR HUBER

he shuffles along the median
clutching his misspelled cardboard sign asking God
    to bless me
I stare ahead willing a green to remove me from
    my discomfort
I drive away
she sits cross legged by the dollar store
cuddling her cat
her hoodie is damp from the rain
her margarine tub contains few coins
she smiles at me
my chest tightens
I hand her my umbrella
the one with the broken prong
I walk away

they appear suddenly on my path by the river amid
    their sagging tents
colourful
yet lacking cheer
an encampment strewn with rust and ruin
they look up from their fire
they call out
good morning
how can it be good
when my running shoes cost more than their dismal dwellings
my guilt and shame well up
are we not our brother's keeper
I hesitate
I turn
I run away

Caravanning

MARY LOU McRAE

I T WAS AUGUST, 1962. I had turned sixteen and my brother, Bruce, would be fourteen in December. Dad wanted to show us other parts of Canada. And what better way to do that than by caravan? He only had two weeks of vacation and because we lived in London, Ontario, he chose Prince Edward Island for our destination.

Because my brother and I bickered constantly, my parents allowed both of us to invite a friend, hoping they would act as a buffer between us. I chose my best friend, Lyn. Bruce and Lyn's brother, Frank, had developed a friendship through us, so Bruce invited Frank. There were eight kids in their family, so sharing wasn't new to them.

Dad would be the only driver on the trip. Through the years, he had attempted to teach Mom. The lessons took place after church, on remote country roads. Mom would slide across the seat to get behind the wheel while Dad walked around to the passenger door. Bruce and I, along with the dog, stayed in the back seat under strict orders to remain quiet. No matter how many lessons Mom had, she always started with, "Now Reg, don't get mad, but what pedal is the gas and which one's the brake?"

After a half hour of the car lurching and slamming to a stop and Bruce and I crashing into the back seat (the days of no seat belts), Dad would say, "Well, that's enough for one day. Maybe we'll try next Sunday." I had just received my beginner's licence and longed for the day I could get behind the wheel.

Dad picked up the rented trailer the Friday before we were to leave. Two bunks in the back for us kids, and the table that converted into a bed for my parents.

Mom held a draw to allow two of us kids to spend the night before we left in the trailer. Lyn and I won. Hunger pains had us opening and closing drawers and cupboards, looking for something to satisfy our cravings. Hidden behind cereal boxes and tinned food we found a Spanish bar cake. Mom made most of her own desserts, but she often found these moist, fruity rectangular cakes with soft icing on the reduced table. We ate the whole thing and hid the offending wrapper in the house garbage.

My parents wanted us on the road early. But with four teenagers to stir and feed, and then wait while we groomed and chose the right outfit to wear, early became 9 a.m.

With directions and hand gestures from the five of us and Wimpy barking encouragement, Dad backed out of the driveway. All our neighbours were out in full force to wish us *Bon voyage*. I'm sure they thanked the Lord they were not my parents.

Three kids sat in the back with the dog. Mom was in the front with the fourth kid wedged between my parents on the bench seat. All us kids took a turn there, but it was usually the child who was causing the biggest commotion that day. The middle kid had the job of plugging in the car lighter and holding the red coils toward the cigarettes clutched between my parents' lips.

We were barely on the open road each day when Dad would start belting out songs in his lovely tenor voice, with the rest of us joining in. What Mom lacked in holding a tune she made up for in volume, usually lagging a few notes behind the rest of us. Their favourite songs were from the musical *Oklahoma*.

I was fascinated by the ever-changing scenery, hills, lakes and rivers. And soon I would see my first mountains in Quebec, and the Atlantic Ocean when we reached the coast. When we came upon a boring stretch, we played card games and taught ourselves to play chess. Rounds of singing and games often continued into the evening around a campfire.

Dad had purchased a Kodak movie camera so we could make a documentary of our holiday. Mom, with a cigarette clenched between her teeth, was in charge of the camera. *Whizz, whizz.* One telephone pole, two telephone poles, and on it went until she had captured rare footage of the poles lining the highway. The swaying of the car soon had her snoozing, the camera on her lap and her head bouncing on her chest. Her cigarette dangled between her false teeth, which had slid down. The kid in the middle front seat would extract the cigarette, trying not to disengage her teeth. And if Dad wasn't looking, inhale on it before butting it in the ashtray.

When we were driving through a particularly scenic spot, Dad would try to rouse Mom. "Lil, you're missing the scenery." But on she slept.

Our first night was near Kingston, where we toured Fort Henry, having left the dog in the trailer. In her sweetest voice, Mom asked the ticket lady for two tickets. "My kids are all under twelve," she said, glancing up at the four of us. The ticket lady just stared. I guess she thought an argument with Mom wasn't worth her summer job, so in we strode.

"Lil, I wish you wouldn't do that," Dad said, when we were inside the gate.

That supper, Mom heated her homemade bite-sized meat pies along with a big pot of baked beans. She started rooting through the cupboards, lifting and moving items. "I'm sure I packed a Spanish bar cake. Frank, Bruce, did you eat it?" she asked.

Dad, always the peacemaker, said, "Well, maybe you forgot it."

Years later, Lyn and I confessed.

Us kids loved nothing more than wandering through gift shops. This usually happened during one of my parents' frequent grocery stops. At one place, Frank and Bruce were busy trying on rings. Frank stood with his right hand extended, admiring a ring. "How much?" he asked, looking toward the shop owner. Ten dollars was the reply—Frank's entire fortune.

He tried to extract the ring, but it wouldn't budge past his knuckle. Sister Lyn got in the act. She pulled and pulled, muttering how stupid he was. Frank's finger had turned from white to purple. He grabbed an aerosol can of shaving lotion and sprayed enough foam over his hand to put out a small forest fire. *Voilà*, the ring slipped off. The proprietor watched this scene with her arms crossed over her ample breasts. "You'll have to pay for that," she said. Frank happily handed over fifty cents for the shaving lotion while returning the mucky ring. He now had ammunition for his first shave, still a few years off.

We voted Bruce's purchase the best. In the back corner of a quirky second-hand store, he spotted a moth-eaten cougar's head. After a bit of haggling, it became his for ten dollars. Over the years, it shuffled locations until it found its forever home on the inside door of the outhouse at our aunt's cottage. We never tired of hearing the squeals of unsuspecting visitors to the throne room.

Mom got a brainwave to collect a tree from every province. Swatting mosquitoes, and accompanied by the dog, us kids scouted the tall grasses that abutted the roads next to the woods, looking for that perfect, symmetrically shaped fir to add to our yard. Mom followed with the shovel. We always dug up several in case one died. We also added colourful, uniquely shaped rocks to start a rock garden.

One time, a crew of labourers were planting saplings along the stretch of highway where we had stopped. "Lil, you can't dig those up, they've just been planted," Dad called out.

"Oh, it's fine, Reg. There are so many. Isn't that right?" Mom said, addressing the planters, who were rendered speechless. Soon, every inch of the trailer floor and our beds were covered in a hodgepodge of containers filled with trees and rocks.

Most of the campsites we stayed at had pit toilets. So, at one recently opened location, we were thrilled when Mom returned from the washroom and announced it was brand new and had flush toilets and showers. "Though the showers are all open and they look like they were designed for midgets," she said.

They were so new that the Men's and Women's signs had not been placed on the doors. What Mom thought were tiny showers were urinals. "Well, how did you girls know that? When were you last in a men's washroom?" Mom asked.

We spent a day touring Quebec City. My parents let us loose with strict dos and don'ts while they took a conducted tour. Lyn and I separated from the boys but had the job of dragging Wimpy along. Wimpy didn't have a leash. Like most canines of that generation, she wandered the neighbourhood with no complaints from passersby and always returned in the evening. We tied to her collar the doubled-over clothesline Mom had brought along, and we were off. We took turns wandering into shops while one of us stayed with the dog. Mom had had all Wimpy's spaniel-like fur shaved off, leaving just a wispy tassel at the end of her tail. One little girl announced, "I know. She's a prairie dog." Poop bags were unheard of, so a few deposits were left for unsuspecting tourists.

Our feet were killing us. We had hiked up and down the narrow, cobbled streets, stopping to watch street entertainers and vendors. It was the hippy generation. The only thing I remember us buying was a package of four cigarillos. Lyn and I thought the hippies looked cool smoking them. Our cigarillo venture turned out to be a blessing. We both turned green and upchucked our lunch, turning us off smoking for life.

When we arrived at Fundy Bay National Park, it was already dark. The boys slid down a steep embankment to the water. It was low tide, and because Fundy has the highest tides in the world, there was a vast expanse of mud flats. Before long, the boys were wrestling, rolling, and throwing mud balls at each other. When they hobbled back to the trailer, we only knew them by the voices coming from their mud-encrusted faces. Wimpy was only slightly more recognizable—but the scent of rotten fish announced her arrival. Bruce reached for the trailer door. "We'll just wash up a bit before supper."

"Over my dead body," Mom replied as she barred the door.

The boys slinked off to use the public washroom, while Lyn and I were given the job of bathing the dog. "Not fair. The boys should have to do this," we said as we screwed up our noses, cornered the dog and sprayed her with the hose.

Our ferry crossing to PEI was an occasion to dress up. The guys wore their sports jackets, and Mom and us girls, our flowered summer dresses with matching cardigans. Lyn's and mine had built-in stiff crinolines that swayed when we walked. We looked quite dapper as we exited the bowels of the ship and headed onto the deck to enjoy the sea air and view. The boys were sauntering along like a pair of peacocks after some twittering girls. This image was shattered when seagulls with perfect aim sent a stream of white down their smart navy jackets.

We had the luxury of three nights at Cavendish Beach. From there, we explored the small island.

Dad introduced us to lobsters. He bought them live from a local fishery while Frank secured a pamphlet on how to eat the crustaceans. Dad plopped them into a huge pot of boiling water on the camp stove. Mom and Bruce just nibbled at theirs while the rest of us, dripping in melted butter, devoured ours and theirs. But no one enjoyed them more than Frank. He even crunched down on some of the shells, devouring them along with the innards.

Every Sunday, we attended church. We were Presbyterians, but denomination didn't matter on holidays. Dad had spotted a white-steepled country church close to our campsite the day before. Sunday morning, dressed in our finery, we headed there, having left the dog in the trailer at our campsite. Mom and Dad led, with Mom offering greetings to the sparse crowd of parishioners, who turned to gawk and whisper, probably wondering who we were visiting. We always sat in the back pew at our church, but that spot was taken, so Mom jammed us into the second-last one. The narrow seat creaked and groaned under our weight and we had to shuffle slightly sideways to fit. Thankfully, Frank and Bruce were at the far end of the pew with Mom and Dad in the middle and me and Lyn on the aisle.

The opening hymn and prayer had finished when all heads turned to the creaking church door. A middle-aged lady entered dressed in a tight-fitting outfit that emphasized her matronly figure. She marched up the aisle, swinging a hymn book in her right hand. Her backless pumps kept missing the narrow blue runner and echoed off the hardwood. A man and three kids, two boys and a girl, trailed behind her. The dour-faced minister stopped his address and waited as they settled themselves right under his nose.

During the offering, the lady hoisted her dress to climb the steep step to the empty choir station at the front of the church. There she opened her hymn book and large mouth and in an ear-splitting voice favoured us with a solo. It was so unexpected that us kids started to snicker, which brought elbowing from Mom and Dad. But what really set us off was when her youngest, dressed in short pants, a jacket and bow tie, turned in the pew he shared with his siblings and father to face the congregation. He had his eyes screwed shut, with his fingers firmly planted in his ears. Oh, how I wanted to do that.

Despite our not-so-reverent presence, we were warmly welcomed at the end of the service. Following lemonade on the lawn, we piled into the car. The engine was dead.

But the gods were with us. One usher was the town's mechanic.

He drove us back to the trailer, then got his tow truck and took the car to his garage. On Monday, he fixed the car, and we were on our way to the ferry and home.

"Reg, do you think you could get a three-week vacation next year, so we could travel to Vancouver Island?" Mom asked.

"Yes, yes," us kids yelled. Dad nodded and Wimpy barked her approval.

Not Just Lonely

BRUCE LORD

the drop of water just
as it falls from the last iceberg

the last dandelion in
a parched field

the remaining leaf
witnessing the autumnal suicide

the last pterodactyl
watching its mate fall

the rose is crushed
lies bruised and battered
      between the pages

the beauty is gone

you were those petals, i
      those thorns

and when you held me
for the very last time, i fear
      i made your fingers bleed

Last Baby

CHRISTINE LANGLOIS

FROM THE SECOND-STOREY window of the maternity ward, Margaret blew kisses down to her three girls as they waved and hopped up and down for warmth in the snowy parking lot. Silhouetted against the late afternoon sun low on the horizon, they were dark cartoon shapes in their nylon snowsuits with the pale pink of their matching toques a splash of colour against the grey snowbanks. She fixed the image in her mind to sketch later.

Margaret stepped away from the window to pick up the baby lying on her hospital bed, snug in a pink receiving blanket. Carefully, so as not to waken her, she held the newborn aloft. The girls waved harder.

Deep in shadow, their father Harvey stood leaning against their Ford wagon in his mine-issue parka with his hands shoved into his pockets. The glowing orange tip of the cigarette between his lips bobbed each time he took a drag. Harvey didn't wave. He was still hurting. "She looks healthy like her sisters" had been all that he could muster, his voice pinched with disappointment, when he'd met his fourth daughter and not his first son.

Now that the girls had seen their new sister, they were eager to get out of the cold and moved toward the car. As Margaret watched the red taillights retreat down the dark road, she wondered if Harvey had remembered the casserole she'd left in the freezer for their supper. Not her problem. For one more night, Harvey was in charge.

Holding the infant to her chest, Margaret headed for the nursery feeling the painful tug of her stitches with every step. As she moved slowly past the nursing station, Ellen, the head nurse, popped up from behind the desk.

"I'll take her." Ellen scooped the child from Margaret's arms. Ellen, a war widow, had ruled the maternity floor since the forties. "We'll keep her in the nursery tonight and let you sleep. You'll be up doing night feeds soon enough."

Margaret smiled her thanks and shuffled back to her room, easing herself carefully onto the bed. Tomorrow, when her milk came in, she'd be feeding on demand. But for tonight, she'd enjoy an evening to herself with her sketchbook and her transistor radio. She turned the radio on low. Then she picked up her sketchbook and HB pencil and quickly sketched the girls in their snowsuits. She hadn't drawn anything in months but her hand moved with confidence. When she'd captured enough detail to turn the sketch into a painting someday, she stopped and flipped back through the book. The girls sprawled on the beach last summer. Harvey and his dad at the kitchen table playing cards, each profile a mirror image of the other. A self-portrait of her own angular face and deep-set eyes. Going over her work grounded her, reminded her of her skill.

A kitchen staffer delivered her supper tray. Before she dug in, she turned up the volume on her radio, already set to the local station, just in time for the six o'clock news.

Dylan's distinctive baritone filled the room. "The meeting between President Kennedy and Prime Minister Diefenbaker is expected to go ahead…" She ignored the words and let his warm familiar voice wash over her.

She felt foolish but she didn't care. Alone in her hospital room, she could indulge her girlish fantasy that things had turned out differently. She could imagine that Dylan—who taught her to jive and do calculus and held her hand on the way to high school every day for three years—sat across from her at supper tonight.

But, just as Dylan was wrapping up the local weather—"Twenty below Fahrenheit overnight"—Ellen arrived holding a little paper cup and a glass of water, interrupting Margaret's daydream.

"Going to be another cold one. Nice to hear Dylan's voice since he came back. You two were an item in high school, right?" the nurse asked.

Margaret pressed her lips into a smile. "Now that's ancient history. What's in the cup?"

"One more night for your little blue pill. If you want more to take home, I can ask Dr. Scott—he has an office full of samples."

"Yes, please."

Her neighbour Sally was right that Valium was like "relaxing on a cloud." But the pill Margaret really wanted was the other pill that all her friends were talking about—the one that would stop the pregnancies. She couldn't mention that to Ellen. The nurse was her mother's age. She would never approve.

Ellen spied Margaret's sketchbook. "Can I take a peek?" Without waiting for an answer, she picked it up and started turning pages. "Good to see you keeping up your little hobby. And your girls are getting so big! How old is your oldest?"

"She just turned six. She started grade one last fall."

"So, you'll only have three at home." Ellen put down the sketchbook and picked up Margaret's empty supper tray. "Now you enjoy your last night of quiet for a bit."

Margaret lay back against her pillows. She'd save the blue pill for later and just enjoy the solitude for now. She stared up at the ceiling panels and the overhead fluorescents and shifted her weight to ease the pain in her back. She replayed her labour in her mind—her water breaking as she stood feeding the wringer washer the last load, her quick call to Sally to pick up the girls, waiting for Harvey to finish his shift and drive her in, then the blur of the wheelchair ride straight into delivery and then pushing, pushing. And then the baby's shrill cry before Dr. Scott announced "another girl" and the nurse carried her off.

"Harvey's going to have to wait for the next one for that son!" Scott had said as he stitched her up.

Thinking about that son made Margaret so sad she was afraid she might weep. Why had they conjured up Billy with his thick brown curls and his solid frame like a miniature Harvey? Billy was the name that Harvey's dad went by, and Harvey had said they would call this child William and Billy for short. Harvey hadn't wanted to jinx it by picking a girl's name in reserve. On her own Margaret had chosen Susan, but she hadn't said anything to Harvey. Now she wished she had. She wished she could have prepared him somehow.

They would come to love Susan as they did her sisters—that's what mothers and fathers do. But Harvey belonged to a world of men where fathers and sons bonded over games of shinny and deer season. He wouldn't give up on that dream. *He will want to try again.*

Margaret rode an afterpain and let that reality sink in. Trying again. Another newborn. The night feedings. The diapers frozen on the line in winter. The small sticky hands endlessly pulling at her. *I can't do it again.* The afterpain eased off and she unclenched her jaw. "I can't do it again," she said out loud to the empty room. Starting today, she would piece her own life back together. If she didn't, she was afraid what might happen to her.

Margaret reached for the tiny blue pill in the paper cup, looking forward to the dreamy, soft-as-a-cloud world she was about to enter. Her muscles slowly relaxed. Dylan's low voice filled the room again and she closed her eyes, all the better to conjure him sitting close beside her. She imagined him reaching for her hand and felt his soft touch deep in her core like another afterpain, except that there was no pain. She thought about that last night they spent together before he left for school in the south.

Dylan's voice interrupted her thoughts. He was signing off for the evening. He was wishing her a good night.

"Goodnight, Dylan," she whispered, remembering the whispered promises when he gave her his ring, the awkward coupling in the cab of his father's pickup, the long goodbye at her front door.

She didn't keep her promise for long. By the time Dylan returned from university at Thanksgiving, she'd already let Harvey walk her home from the bar a couple of times after her shift and she hadn't cared who saw them together. Harvey had graduated the year before, starting underground at the mine and living with some buddies. He had broad shoulders and muscular arms under his plaid shirts and a wallet full of cash that he generously opened often at the bar. When he turned his attention to her, she was flattered and nervous. Dylan was just a kid like her but Harvey was a man.

When Dylan came to see her, she acted as if she hardly knew him. She didn't ask him about school. He didn't mention Harvey. Instead, he said he'd realized he needed to be independent to focus on his schooling. She'd offered no resistance and quickly slipped off his ring, relieved that she wasn't the one who had to end it. By Christmas, she and Harvey were engaged. When they were married the following summer, she was already three months pregnant with Linda.

But now, eight years later, she tried to understand how it all happened. During the last year of high school, why did she watch Dylan make his dream happen while she accepted hers as stillborn? He was so excited when he got his letter from Ryerson Polytechnic in Toronto. "Come with me. You still have time and your marks are good enough." It was true. A few other girls with good marks had already been accepted at teachers' college and nursing school. But she wasn't interested in either of those choices. Her choice should have been art school. She loved drawing and painting the way Dylan loved radio. But sketching friends' portraits and painting posters to advertise Friday night sock hops didn't seem enough to qualify her to go to a big-city school. Besides, she had no idea what she'd do with an art degree if she got one. *I wasn't sure I could do it so I just drifted.*

She could feel herself slipping away into sleep. The word "bliss" floated through her mind. She would ask Dr. Scott for more blue pills in the morning, when he came to sign her out. And maybe she'd screw up her courage and ask for the other pill too. Why shouldn't she?

Margaret sat gingerly on the chair in her hospital room with Susan in her arms. She could hear the doctor's booming voice as he came down the hall. "Big game tonight!" he called to someone. Scott's son played goal for the local Junior team and the doctor, in his distinctive raccoon coat on his six-foot frame, was a loud and unmissable spectator at every game.

"Well, Margaret—it looks like you're ready to make tracks," he said when he arrived at her door to sign her out. "How's Harvey? I hear he's still playing for the mine team?"

"He's signed up for another year."

"Good for him—any questions before I sign you out?"

"I was wondering…about those pills I had for sleeping?"

"Ellen already mentioned—I've left her the samples and 'script."

Then Margaret surprised herself. "Thanks, and also I'm wondering…well, I'm not sure really that…the thing is I'm wondering about the birth control pill."

She could see that Dr. Scott was surprised too. His face lost its smile and his eyes widened slightly. For a second, he seemed at a loss. Then he quickly recovered.

"Well, well, well. That's a big decision, little lady. I always recommend to new mothers that they not be too hasty in these things.

I'm not sure Harvey is ready to give up on that defenceman, are you? Why don't you two talk it over and then we can revisit in a few months."

He didn't wait for her response. He smiled and nodded, as if to say the matter was settled.

Harvey came through the door bringing cold air with him. He brushed snow out of his hair and off his coat.

"She's ready to go," Scott said. He gave Margaret a wink to let her know her secret was safe and patted Harvey on the shoulder as he turned to leave the room.

Margaret stared at the two men. Her chest felt tight and her face got hot. "Dr. Scott!" she shouted to the man's retreating back.

The doctor turned around, his eyebrows raised.

"I've decided I want that prescription. I'll get it at my six-week appointment." She could hear a shake in her voice.

Harvey furrowed his brow and looked from Margaret to the doctor.

Scott's face hardened into a professional mask. "We can discuss that." He walked out, with a nod to Harvey and a knowing look. *Your wife's a little emotional.*

Harvey looked back at her. "Are you okay? What's going on?"

Margaret's face flushed with embarrassment, even shame, but this time her voice didn't shake.

"This baby is my last. I'm asking Scott for the birth control pill."

Harvey kept his own voice even as if he was talking to one of their girls. "This isn't the time to be talking about that. Let's get you home."

"It *is* time! I've made my choice."

Ellen came through the door pushing a wheelchair, choosing to ignore the tension in the small room. "Hop in and I'll push you down to the car."

When Margaret was safely in the passenger seat with Susan

on her lap, Ellen leaned in. "I almost forgot. Here's that 'script and some samples to get you through the next few nights."

Margaret waved them away. "Never mind. I've changed my mind."

The nurse pulled back, surprised. "Suit yourself. They're here if you need them."

Harvey put the car in gear and pulled out of the parking lot into the gathering snowstorm. He didn't say anything more about what she'd said at the hospital, but Margaret didn't expect him too. He needed time. But she'd told him—that was what mattered.

Staring out at the snow now falling in thick clumps, Margaret still felt weepy. Then she remembered that she always felt weepy after a baby. But this time, she also felt lighter, clearer. She looked down at her newborn's tiny perfect face. When Susan started school, Margaret would be thirty-one. Not young but not old either. She'd use these next few years to figure out what to do next. She gently stroked her infant's soft cheek. Tomorrow, she'd find a few minutes to sketch her—her last baby.

Master

LAURIE BROWNE

There was a time
when I'd smother
your face
with a thousand
kisses
and
my love
was sure-footed
and
strong.
Just a young one
so eager
to please.
I thought that we would
always
walk
side by side.

I was not prepared
for your

Pavlovian plans
to keep me
at your
heels.
Attempts at defiance
were quickly
quelled
by the short, choking
pulls
designed to leave me
gasping.
The tether
became
tighter
the greater
the escapes.

Now, I lie
on a foundation
of dirt
and
stones,
with my eyes
lowered
and
my ears
flattened.
I twitch
and
whimper
in my sleep,
dreaming
of a different
fate.

Not the one

that you might think—
surrounded by
children
and
playful
belly rubs.
I do not want
to rely
on table scraps,
only
to become
complacent,
fat
and
lazy.
I imagine
that I am immersed
in tall grass,
running
at full speed.
My tongue
panting
unabashedly,
from a mouth
wide open
and
full of
froth.
I am one
with my new pack—
Feral,
insatiable
and
wonderfully
wild.

The Idels in March

DONNA COSTA

1. Maggie

WE'RE GETTING A dog! I can't believe Mom finally said yes. I've been begging since forever. She always said a dog was a lot of work, a big responsibility, that I was too young. Whatever. I just turned ten and finally she said I was grown-up enough to have one.

I get to pick it out from the kennel tomorrow. Should I get a small dog, all cuddly and cute? Or a big dog that can play Frisbee? It would be fun to have the kind that wears ribbons in her hair and pretty dog coats. I hope she'll like me as much as I already like her and I haven't even picked her out yet. She'll be a friend for forever and ever.

Mom says I have to walk the dog and feed it and take care of it. No problem! Picking up dog poo is gross, but I guess I'll get used to it. My friend showed me how to put my hand in the bag so I never get guck on my fingers. I had to wipe my own barf once. I guess scooping poo will be easier than that.

2. Oliver

A dog! I can't believe my mom is getting my sister a dog. She'll probably get one of those sissy dogs named Precious or Poopsie or Trinket and carry her in a front pack like a baby. If only it was a real dog like Killer or Butch or Demonspawn, something that drools and licks its own balls. Ha, that would be cool!

It's her dog, so I don't get a say at all. Which really frosts *my* balls. I begged for a dog and was told no so many times I stopped asking. Doesn't mean I stopped wanting one. I'm just not a whiner and a baby like my kid sister. Maybe I should be. Seems that's how you get things around here. Not by getting good grades or doing chores. I've cut the grass, shovelled the snow and taken out garbage countless times. Yet she's the one who gets a dog.

Which means I have to hate it on principle. What can I do to torment it?

Maybe I can get a cat. One that hisses and scratches sissy dogs. Cats are smart, dogs are dumb. Cats are way cooler. Yeah, I'll keep working on Mom now that she's softened the No Pets rule.

3. Dad

I can't believe Elise told Maggie she could have a dog! Did she forget I have allergies? That I have asthma? What the hell. She told Maggie she can pick whatever dog she wants. She could at least have told her to get a non-shedding breed. I bet Maggie would like a cute little Maltese or toy poodle. I hope Maggie doesn't get one of those dogs with eye snot. Gross! Or one that slobbers with strings of disgusting drool that flap from side to side when it shakes its head.

No matter what Maggie gets, my allergies are going to flare up and I'll be sniffing antihistamines endlessly. Elise has no idea what it's like to feel as if you can't breathe—to have eyes so itchy, you have to rub, but it's like sand scratching your eyeballs when you do and then they ooze gunk from the corners.

No way that dog is sleeping in our bed either. Not even when

Maggie has a nightmare and wants to sleep with us. Our bedroom is off-limits to dogs! No dogs on the couch either. I don't want dog hair floating into the popcorn on family movie night.

What was Elise thinking? I always suspected she thinks I just like to whine about my sinuses. Getting a dog proves she has no sympathy for me at all.

～

In bed late at night, Robert and Elise finally talked. She claimed that of course she had every intention of guiding Maggie toward a non-shedding dog.

"You know Maggie's always been a Daddy's girl. Just the slightest hint about making you sniffle and she'll be steered in the right direction."

"You still should have discussed it with me first," Robert grumbled.

"I'm sorry. I got caught up in the moment."

"And what about Oliver? He always wanted a dog."

"Ollie?" Elise said. "He hasn't asked in ages. I figured he was over that phase."

"He wouldn't say anything to you, but I know he was crushed."

"Well, it'll be everyone's dog anyway. It'll be part of the family, won't it?"

"It's not the same and you know it," Robert protested.

"Ollie needs to learn to speak up. How was I supposed to know?"

The bed squeaked as Robert turned onto his side away from Elise and pulled the fleece blankets up to his stubbly chin. *You'd know if you were home more often. You'd know if you spent time with the kids, instead of throwing a new computer game at them or another bloody activity that I have to take them to because you're too busy.*

Elise rolled onto her side, her back to Robert. *Bloody hell. I try to do a good deed and now he's mad. So, I forgot for a moment about his allergies. It wasn't intentional. And I had no clue Ollie still wanted a dog. At least Maggie is happy. At least somebody in this house is happy.*

Elise wished she could turn on her cell phone and check her emails, but she knew Robert was still awake.

After returning home with Elise, Maggie placed an extra-small dog crate on the family room carpet. As soon as she unlatched the door, a tiny canine jumped into Maggie's arms. Maggie turned to face Ollie. "Well, what do you think?"

"A Chihuahua? That's the dumbest dog ever," Ollie said. "I suppose you're going to dress it up in ribbons and frilly dresses?"

"No, I'm not. Cuz it's a boy," Maggie explained.

"Elise, don't Chihuahuas shed?" Robert asked.

"It's such a tiny dog, how much can it shed really?" Elise asked.

"That's right, Daddy, it hardly has any hair, so I have to put a coat on him when he goes outside in the winter."

"I *knew* she'd be dressing it up." Oliver threw his hands up in disgust. "So sappy. Just like a doll."

"No, it's not. I told you, he's a boy." Maggie pulled the dog's wardrobe out of the bag—a denim jacket, a leather coat with a faux fur collar, a skull and crossbones hoodie with a punk Mohawk fringe, bright red.

"At least it's better than ribbons," Oliver conceded. "What's his name?"

"Well, I picked him out, so I thought you could name him," Maggie offered.

Robert looked at Elise. They both looked at Oliver, who was pleased but trying not to show it.

"Brutus!" Oliver announced.

"You like that name?" Maggie asked the dog. He licked her face and Maggie giggled. "Okay…Brutus."

Maggie carried the dog, giving Brutus a tour of the house. They put a padded dog bed in Maggie's room and one in the family room. When she finally set him on the floor, he sniffed around before lifting his leg and peeing on Elise's sheepskin slipper.

Robert sneezed and, with a sigh, headed to the medicine cabinet for his decongestant.

After weeks of breaking in the family, Brutus had his routine. When Maggie went to bed, he would snuggle beside her on the ruffled pillow. When Oliver went to sleep later, Brutus would ditch Maggie and settle with Ollie amid the teen odours—hockey sweat, yeasty feet and pizza breath—where he stayed until morning.

Maggie didn't always remember to let Brutus out for his morning business, but Brutus learned that Elise would let him out if he didn't ease up on his whining. He'd peed enough times on her footwear—and only hers—that he could depend on her speedy attention to his needs.

Once, Maggie doled too much food into his metal dish and when Elise tried to take it away, Brutus snarled and bared his teeth. Elise pulled back, not daring to get between him and his bowl. For good measure, he crapped in her new leather shoe, then hid in Oliver's room where Elise would never find him.

4. Elise

I can't believe I let Maggie get a dog. What was I thinking! That damn dog hates me. He snarls at me. He pees in my slippers. He even crapped in my new Bottega loafers. As soon as I sit down, he's there. Humping my foot, my leg. He even jumped up on my lap, then tried to hump my hand. Maggie said he was trying to dance with me. So disgusting!

I was the one who brought him home from the kennel. I'm the one who buys his food, takes him to the vet, lets him out most mornings. And what thanks do I get? I hate him as much as he hates me.

Thank God Robert insisted no dogs in our bedroom. If Brutus ever got in there, I'm certain he'd deliberately pee, or worse, on my side of the bed. I'm not taking any chances, so I keep the bedroom door closed at all times. Oliver fusses over the damn dog almost as much as Maggie. Robert too, even though it makes him sneeze and then he comes to bed snorting and making all kinds of disgusting noises because he's stuffed up.

Maybe what we need is a cat?

❧

Robert, Oliver and Maggie huddled together on the leather sofa on family movie night. Brutus was curled on Maggie's lap while Oliver and Robert took turns tossing popcorn to Brutus and scratching behind his ears with every successful catch.

Elise arrived home from work, late as usual. *They don't even acknowledge I'm home. What happened to running to the door to hug me? What happened to being happy to see me?* She took a seat in the brocade wing chair, placing her red leather Valextra bag on the floor and a small cage on the other side.

"I have a surprise for all of you," Elise said.

Maggie clapped. "I love surprises!"

As Robert paused the movie, Elise opened the door of the cage.

"Pssst, pssst," she called. Out sauntered a pale grey sphynx cat with large ears edged in black.

"Meet Duchess." Elise lifted the feline onto her lap and began stroking her hairless chamois skin.

"But, Mommy, she's… naked," Maggie said.

"That is one ugly cat!" said Oliver.

"Non-shedding, I presume," Robert said.

"I thought of you when I bought it, darling."

Robert, Maggie and Oliver stared, but did not reach out to pet the hairless creature. Duchess eyed Brutus until he began quivering on Maggie's lap. Elise noticed and set Duchess on the arm of the wing chair so the cat could get a better look at Brutus. She flattened her ears to the side like a gremlin, then arched her back and hissed. Teeth glaring, she dug her claws into the armrest.

"Nice kitty." Elise smiled and scratched Duchess behind the ears with her long, red nails.

5. Duchess

Battle lines have been drawn—Elise and me versus The Others. They all refuse to touch my soft, supple skin and the master bedroom is a No Pet Zone, so I'm not privy to battles that occur there.

After Brutus slips from Maggie's room to Oliver's, I roam the house. First, I play with the mutt's chew toys. I prefer things I can swat, but I did once pounce from the kitchen chair onto Brutus' squeaky rabbit just to see him come running because I dared to touch *his* property. So my sharp teeth sometimes put holes in his squeak toys. Oopsie.

When Robert isn't looking, I gnaw the electrical wires. I can't resist. If I close my eyes, the vibrations feel like the pounding heart of a captured mouse, fear coursing through its body before I kill it.

I learned how to turn on the water in the bathroom so I can enjoy a *fresh* drink, not that tepid liquid in my dish with dog hair in it. I can't turn the tap off, so I make sure to drink after Oliver uses the bathroom. He takes the blame for the dripping faucet. Is it my fault they left me for a whole day and the water overflowed, ruining the drywall and the ceiling below?

꙳

Oliver and Maggie leaned against the sofa playing video games while Brutus simpered at their feet. Between game battles, they tossed a plush squiggly ball for Brutus to fetch. They ignored Duchess, curled up in her blankets, until she stood up, retching and gagging.

"Something's wrong with Duchess," Maggie said.

Oliver glanced over. "Probably just a hairball."

"She doesn't have any hair," Maggie said. "Maybe you should see if her nose is hot."

"That's dogs, you dolt," Ollie said, tapping on his remote, focusing on the game. "And I'm not touching that *thing*."

Later, when everyone was asleep, Duchess stood in the hallway outside their bedroom doors. She coughed up some cat grass, then lay on her side, mewing.

Brutus emerged from Oliver's room, sniffing the cat and the spew. *Mew, mew.*

But like the others, Brutus walked away.

Et tu, Brutus?

But he'd already slipped back into Oliver's room.

6. Brutus

I hear Duchess still mewing, each whimper becoming weaker. Maybe she really is sick? I jump from Ollie's bed, dashing into the hallway. She's still on the floor beside her green hurl, shivering without blankets or fur.

It's my chance to be a canine hero! I begin barking to alert the family, then scratch on the master bedroom door. Elise arrives first and scoops Duchess into her arms.

"Something's wrong with Duchess!" Elise shouts and begins crying. The others appear, rubbing their eyes and yawning. "I've got to get her to emergency. Maggie, hold Duchess while I get dressed."

"I don't want to…" Maggie says, but Elise has already thrust Duchess into her arms. "Oh! Oh, she really is soft!" Then Maggie, *my* Maggie, begins stroking that hairless beast. It was the unkindest cut of all. "Poor, poor Duchess."

Even Ollie reaches out a finger to pet her. "She *is* soft. Like a pussy willow," he says.

They fawn over her, bundling her in blankets, cradling her in their arms. Duchess raises her head slightly. Was that a glint in her icy blue eyes?

The last thing I see as they rush out the door is Duchess flicking the tip of her rat-like tail in my direction.

The family gathered around the metal bars where Duchess lay on a blanket on the cage floor.

"Mrs. Idel, Duchess is still groggy from surgery," the vet said. "I removed an item from her tummy. It looked like a squeaker from a chew toy. Good thing you brought her in when you did."

"Duchess," Maggie said. "Brutus saved your life! Now you have to be friends."

Friends? Never! Duchess' tail twitched as she plotted foul deeds and dreadful things to let slip the dogs of war.

Stumped

CHARLOTTE H. BROADFOOT

Oooph. No best kind, wha b'y?

CONSCIOUSNESS SLOWLY RETURNED. Fuzzy, thick tongue roved over split, parched lips. Not enough spittle to hock a loogie, second nature after a binge. Tentative body movements, much restricted.

"Whatta y'at?" Mackie mumbled to himself, struggling to get mind and body working on the same page. Finally: "G'wan. I comes to recall…a scuff." Groan. "Och. Feelin' it; feckin' ribs!"

The seedy old gaffer minded now ("Blow") Torchy and ("Meat") Hook pummelling his face and body with both fists: *the both of 'em hauling off, picking m'self up, all t'ree of us crab-walkin' to Hook's rusty brown Buick sedan and tossing me in the boot.* Impossible to forget Torchy's menacing tone, slamming shut the trunk door overhead, "Should know the drill by now, Mackie. Enjoy the ride!"

Now fully awake, the scruffy, snaggle-toothed East Coaster lamented softly in the pitch dark, "B'y, I knows I were stun," admitting sheepishly to expected outcomes, being a card-carrying member of both the Angels and The Choice from way back.

He found himself reminiscing now on a very green Malcolm Dawe who, long ago, failing to find gainful employment "away" (in an era of politically incorrect Newfie jokes) fell into a murkier lifestyle under various biker banners, scuttling around the less populated areas of Ontario and Quebec. Aging eventually out of club enforcement and demoted to muling in his latter years, he'd been crewing with a splinter chapter: The Axe-L's. Running lucrative drugs in their designated territory—the northern Ontario and USA border at Pigeon Crossing—meant members pulled their weight, "or else."

Hates to say, but the arse is gone out of 'er for me. No point, I knows, sawin' on olden times. Best get on the go. Sighing, Mackie reflected on the current situation. *Be a ways north b'now f'r shore*—a sound reckoning based on the vehicle's severe pitching on deeply rutted roads.

Arh, feckin' hell. A low groan escaped as a battered, bruised hip came into contact with the spare wheel compartment. *Can't let 'em knows I'se woke,* he realized. He could hear muffled voices from the interior of the car as it was, so they'd hear him samesy if he bleated loud enough.

Fully alert now, Mackie took stock. Despite a cracked crystal, the old timepiece on his wrist with Indiglo had taken a lickin' but kept on tickin'. Rheumy grey eyes squinting hard, he could *just* read the dial and used the faint glow to have a look about the tight compartment.

Gawdy! No latch on the inside of this here bus. (Mackie'd assisted Hook in the past with the odd "disposal"—the sedan's trunk *still* smelled rank.) *Trussed like a GD pig, I am.* Silver furnace duct tape bound him hand and foot but in the front, not the back—a stroke of luck!

Suddenly inspired, he scrabbled with bound fists for the old macho, serrated shark's-tooth ornament he'd worn on a chain around his neck since his induction long ago into the Hells Angels (it was a common "fashion" accessory among the ranks of Satan's

Choice back in the day, too). Gripping it securely between his own gummy teeth, Mackie began working it against the wrist-ties. *Now she's goin'! Fire it up laddio.*

The foot bindings proved slightly more difficult. *Shite!* Mackie went at it, wielding the tooth now in a life-and-death frenzy. Finally freeing his feet, he felt a bit woozy—the effects of intense activity and dwindling oxygen working on him, never mind his earlier alcohol content. Leaning back, he paused to gather strength and wits.

Shifting again his small frame within the cramped quarters, the hostage wobbled onto his knees. Congealing blood trickled down over his eyes from various small cuts, clouding his vision. He wiped his face down with the dirty, frayed cuffs of his outerwear to see better. From his wristwatch—he knew roughly when they'd grabbed him—he gauged they'd been on the road two hours. In no time, they'd reach their destination. ("Disposals" were discretionary, but one site within a two-hour radius of Thunder Bay was the hands-down favourite.)

Thoughts swirled. Deemed a "shrivelled-faced old fart," Mackie'd become the whipping boy of the younger, cannibalistic hyenas coming up, hungrily watching him drift lower to the outer periphery of the org. Ageism in biker gangs? Same as everywhere else. No help from that quarter.

One major mistake. In the past he'd held Third Tier status in the Angels, but he boasted when in his cups, to anyone who'd listen, the claim of Second Tier. Believing and spouting the lie himself for ages eventually brought down real Second Tiers on his head—hence his being loaned permanently to the lesser band, the Axe- L's. Regressing to grunt status (*"like a ruddy new b'y"*), he gophered for beer and weed with occasional gigs in disposal assists and "maintenance." With such demotions, Mackie, recollecting The Oath—*BLOOD IN, BLOOD OUT*—could see the ominous writing on the wall.

An injustice still rankled, however, from a decade previous.

(*"For the honour of the club, Mackie!"*) As designated fall guy for First Tier Ricky Soletti ("Knuckles"), he'd served time at Warkworth in lieu of aforesaid arsehole pimp and trafficker (human and drugs). Back then Mackie thought the prison sentence and sacrifice would buy him valuable street cred in the org. *Like hell. Nada. Dispensable.*

Concluding that his long-time loyalty and service to the gangs—whatever *their* take—had earned him the right to one or more of the precious delivery packets, Mackie had planned to move out west and distribute the prime merch himself piecemeal; enjoying his last few years on a sort of pension.

Mackie's prosaic logic and subsequent actions had not impressed the Axe-L's current Road Captain, Sammy "Scissors." It was Sammy's job to maintain both internal order and the pipeline. Stealing, especially by a low-ranking club member, demanded swift and appropriate retribution. A hit was issued on "Lackey Mackie" (the club's mocking moniker) directly after the valuable parcel went missing. They'd found the flunky embarrassingly quickly, despite his moving from location to location, drunkenly trying to keep a step beyond. *Stun to hit the bars,* the captive lamented after the fact. Or had someone ratted? *What odds, eh Mackie?*

Well, that was the least of his problems at this point. *It is where y'at.* Mackie rubbed his grizzled chin whiskers. He knew from experience where some of the preferred "waste management" sites were located. *GD lumber tracks! The shocks on this bus? Narn, left to Hook, the ijit.* The rough journey indicated they were taking him to the northernmost dump. Time was running out...

The thought was father to the deed. Suddenly, wheels came to an abrupt halt in a spray of churned gravel. Focusing, Mackie concentrated on the sounds outside— doors slamming shut; muffled, raspy voices advertising short ornery tempers: "...way too long... Sammy...the little shit!"

How to go in out of it? Mackie strained his ears, trying to catch their movements, anticipating launching himself at his captors as soon as the trunk opened up—maybe get the element of surprise on his side?

On execution, he did startle somewhat his burly leather-vested captors, but lightweight that he was (in all respects) his lunging leap landed only one tough roughly on the ground—the breath temporarily knocked out of him—while the other was barely buffeted to the side of the auto, quickly recovered and fumbled for his gun.

Mackie bolted, hightailing it straight into northern Ontario's boreal forest (notable, he'd once been told by "Brains" Foley, for its 44 billion trees storing 11% of the world's carbon and its 150,000 lakes). Shots whizzed by. Without turning his head, keeping low but stumbling over the rough terrain, Mackie ran deep into the shadows.

The sound of Torchy and Hook's initial bushwhacking quickly faded. Mackie had the advantage over his pursuers' beer bellies and flat feet: *"Why walk a block when you can ride a Hog?"* Scrambling up inclines, dodging fallen trees and rocky outcrops took its toll, but he was proud of his prowess in the circumstances.

When he judged it safe enough, he stopped and took a breather. *It's a mausy day, no lie.* The sudden chill in the air reminded the fugitive it was late October. Like in his birthplace, cold mists would be coming in soon—the precursor to early snows in the north.

He listened intently for the sound of broken twigs, disturbed critters…zero. A weighty silence reigned. The forest had closed protectively over him, and he was appreciative. Mackie smiled for the first time that day.

Wily, on the go again, he changed directions: zigging then zagging. When at last he finally stopped for a full rest, he considered his options. The afternoon light was waning; night would be falling before too long.

Mackie figured Torchy and Hook had quickly returned to their car, waiting a spell to see if the escapee would take the chance of coming back to the only roadway in miles, such as it was. Mackie knew he wasn't going to do *that;* that would be suicide, even if he knew which way to go in the first place. The hoods wouldn't wait around too long, though, he was sure.

Feck it. He scratched the back of his head where Hook had koshed him, bringing him down outside that Fourth Street bar. Looking around, Mackie tried to concentrate. *I t'inks those b'ys'll be gone b' now. They'll be for finding t'nearest bar and tank up.* Relieved. *Long as I ner show face again in TB, I's'll be alright.*

Torchy and Hook could rest easy too, since they'd recovered his stash—turned it over to Sammy, winning points. No way would they spill on a botched disposal. *So, me cocky. We's came in on a road, so's we'll goes out on a road. Find one soon, f'r shore. Go west after dat.*

As night fell, a bruised and hungry Mackie burrowed into the recessed split of a rock face for the night. *B'y, I shore could do wid a Jiggs dinner, I'se that gut-founded.* He'd broken off some evergreen branches for cover as well as insulation. In fall, evenings in the north got wintry. He shivered. While his heart raced his brain followed suit, thoughts bouncing around, taking him back decades.

I ner should've joined up wid "Harley" Davis on "collections." The younger, naive Malcolm soon learned what the term entailed: roughing up down-on-their-luck gamblers or small business owners late on protection-pay instalments. Harley favoured baseball bats and tire irons. Once Mackie'd got the hang of it though, he didn't shirk either; it was just a job like any other—put food and drink on his table. Sometimes out of sympathy however, Mackie asked the frightened stooge for input—which joint was to be sacrificed: ankle, elbow, knee or hip. Mackie winced in recollection. He was hardly an innocent—more an accessory *before* the fact.

"But I ner kilt no one," he said, defending himself out loud to his boreal audience, following angrily with: "Shore, and all I did for 'em? Jus a lousy mark for that arsehole Knuckles to use of…"

The long night wore on. Mackie's stomach grumbled loudly. He hadn't been too worried at first, figuring getting far enough away from his pursuers was *the main t'ing*. As soon as dawn broke, however, he took stock. *Now* he was anxious.

All the scruffy little Newfoundlander could see were towering, cone-laden trees. And where there weren't any, brackish swamp or granite rock. He did a 360 but had no idea of the direction he'd come, much less where civilization might lie. And: *Where is all d'em GD boreal lakes?* He needed clean water to wash the crust off himself. Drink. Eat. *But first, I'se got to piss…*

As luck would have it, a sleety drizzle began to fall shortly afterward. His grey hoodie, plaid cotton flannel shirt underneath, thin holey socks, track pants and old trainers were soon soaked. Plunging on through the forest, the hope was to find a stream or river he could follow somewhere… anywhere. The boreal wasn't quite so welcoming now, conifers blocking out the sky itself half the time.

Mackie coloured up like one big bruise. By the end of the second day, after choosing a direction and forging on, he'd begun to shiver. At first, he thought he could shrug off the cold and damp, but as he grew increasingly foggy-brained, critical decisions got harder. He needed more breaks too, as he climbed with escalating difficulty over forest detritus and rocky cliffs. Even if he got to the top of a hill, an unending green horizon stymied any directional commitment. If the sun wasn't shining, east could be west, or north, or south.

Night came again, and with it a steep drop in temperature and fear of roving wild animals. The b'ys had gone and emptied out his pockets after thrashing him, so no lighter or smokes. He tried half-heartedly the old Indian trick of rubbing sticks together. *Feckin' fire!* Just try to find any dry twigs to light, even if he'd managed a flame. He didn't have the energy anyway. Instead, he bundled himself again under a spreading spruce's branches, and tried to pile on a blanket of leaves. A sleep of exhaustion overtook him eventually.

By the third morning, Mackie found himself stiff as a board, feverish and clammy. Temperatures in the night plummeting to four degrees, his internal core temperature followed suit. Munching on spruce tips resulted in gagging. He was afraid to try fungi. Hunger and thirst had been a constant, but were somehow muted now. Blurry eyesight accompanied by the thrumming of a constant headache didn't quite divert from teeth chattering like a jackhammer in his ears. Exhausted, frozen to the core—yet he felt compelled unnaturally to unzip his hoodie, pull it off, and drop it behind him as he rose.

Forcing himself up in this last monumental effort, Mackie stood on shaky pins for a few minutes. Befuddled, eventually he put one foot in front of the other, walking aimlessly in no particular direction. After a time, he couldn't help but notice: *B'y, I t'ought I seen that stump befores?*

The bewildered Newfie stopped in his tracks, wavering. He just wanted to find a hollow and lie there for a spell. *A short nap, and then, f'r it again.*

A rocky overhang beckoned, and he lay down beneath it. Mist descended like a cold, wet shroud. It occurred to him that no one would be missing him enough to report him "missing"—certainly not his club mates.

A lethargic Mackie pulled himself into the fetal position for warmth. Eyes leaden, his lashes fluttered futilely against the season's first tiny falling snowflakes. Frigid insides and out prompted drowsy ramblings: *Be dropping over The Rock by and by, so I will. Yarn to tell, too right.* Long breath, softly, *'N plenty of fish…*

Through half-shut eyes he felt the dark army of trees close ranks over him, eventually bending with the cold winds and sweeping him up in their long, needly limbs.

Watching a Man in a Retirement Home Parking Lot

BRENDA MARTIN

He paces doggedly,
artfully dodging imperfections
in the uneven pavement,
sparring with blithe spirits
that haunt the autumn breeze.
One spry step follows another,
just a whisper of a left-leg limp
yet sure-footed rain or shine,
as he counts jabs — one, two, three —
and steps — forty-four, forty-five —
and years — eighty-six, eighty-seven.
Now eighty-eight,
he circuits the lot
in a fight to stay fit,
fit enough to shadow-box,
to dodge perilous potholes,
to pace doggedly.

Wear a Denim Shirt for Me

DIANE KIRBY

I HAVE LIVED A life steeped in denim. My love affair with this material began in the sixties. From the moment I first tried on a pair of blue jeans in a department store dressing room, I was a devotee. Not only was it my favourite colour, but the heavy stiffness of the fabric appealed to me. It provided a sense of structure and grounding, which morphed into comfort as the denim relaxed and became more form-fitting with wear.

As a teenager, I paired my embroidered jeans with smock tops and ribbons in my hair. By the seventies, denim designs exploded. It seemed as if almost everyone owned a denim jacket, some more stylish than others. Mine, as I recall, had colourful patches reflecting matters important to me. By the eighties, I was routinely clad in tailored jeans with silk sweaters, the unofficial uniform of young mothers in my Vancouver neighbourhood. Several years later, I wore them to law school classes paired with tweed blazers. Of course, there were other outfits for specific activities. Working, leisure pursuits and Friday night dates each called for distinct apparel. But the fallback was always jeans, and sometimes by necessity. For, if date night involved a motorcycle ride, a sundress and dressy sandals were not an option. It was jeans, boots and possibly chaps. To this day, jeans remain my go-to clothing.

The denim in my life was not limited only to apparel. Jeans also formed the basis for strong opinions, creativity and memories. I recall my mother stating quite heatedly that she would do my laundry but was "not washing jeans." It might have been her line in the sand against the counter-culture shenanigans sweeping through her household. I also recall my late husband David gifting a pile of worn-out jeans to a friend who promptly crafted a finely tailored denim jacket on her treadle sewing machine. And I will never forget the day we went to a beach town and I wore three pairs of jeans before we reached our destination. I ripped the seat out of the first pair when we went horseback riding, necessitating the purchase of a new pair. As we rode out of town on a motorcycle, I suddenly felt David hitting my calf; my pant leg was in flames. (Contact with hot muffler pipes can do that.) We returned to town, where I purchased an identical second pair not one hour after my previous purchase.

David wore jeans, too. He wore them to work in the automotive trade. He always had a roster of at least a dozen pairs in his dresser, and a couple of new pairs in the closet just in case he needed to go somewhere in "clean" jeans. When he was not working, he was building and racing cars. When not in a fire suit, again, he was in jeans. And he wore them mostly with T-shirts. But when a long sleeve was required, he often wore a denim shirt. Some of the shirts were more faded than others. Some had pearl snaps, others did not. I had no preference. I just loved the look of him in any denim shirt. Now, I admit he cleaned up nicely, with his lifelong trim figure. He could carry anything very well—from a tailored suit to Bermuda shorts with linen shirts. But he came alive when he wore denim. He was simply a vision with his long hair and moustache and the glint in his eye. To almost anyone else, it was just a look that suited him, as if he might have been born to wear those clothes. To me, however, it was a look that bared his soul. And it called out to me. For me, going into those denim-clad arms was going home.

Ironically, despite my preferring David in a denim shirt, I have very few photographs of him wearing one. I know that is because pictures taken back in the day were usually only taken at special family gatherings or vacation spots—places where he dressed specifically for the occasion. But it does not matter because… I remember. I can close my eyes and see him wearing those shirts. I can imagine the softness of the denim surrounding me as he hugs me. Sometimes in my dreams, I can genuinely feel it. I am aware of his love as it radiates through the fabric. I can sense the grounding and peacefulness that comes from the familiarity of the denim and from belonging—to a place, a time, another soul. Those denim shirts and all they mean to me are seared into both my mind's eye and my heart.

And so, I wonder. I wonder how people on the other side of the veil present to each other. How do they present to us? For example, are they just a piece of white light or some shape-shifting form of energy? Or do they take a human form others recognize and remember? Do they project an image of themselves in clothes? Most importantly, when they come to meet us when we pass over, are they identifiable to us by sight? I do hope so.

And I want to tell him, "When it is my time, and you come to meet me, wear a denim shirt for me."

And I will remind him, "If you don't have one, help yourself to one of your old ones still hanging on the back of my closet door."

Dust—An Ode

J. EDWARD ORCHARD

I used to treat it as an enemy,
    a thing to be vanquished on site, wherever it was found
    a soiler, a defiler
    head demon of the unclean

I would hunt it like a man possessed,
    didn't want to be that guy, that walking stereotype
    just another bachelor in a hovel
    just another typical man in a dirty house

Dust. Dust. I still flinch at the sound of the word:
    "Dry dirt in the form of powder that covers surfaces"
    it conjures images of stagnation, of neglect

I could never stay ahead of it,
    Dust is like laundry
    there's always more

Day after day, sweeping, scouring,
    no floor untouched, no countertop untarnished
    it was too much for one man

As I sit here in my father's house,
        my house now…
        I see it; it's found me again

It is here that I realize I've been approaching things all wrong,
        trying too hard
        seeking to scrub my soul of hurt

In fighting it, I was fighting my own grief,
        cleansing my guilt
        trying to heal the wound of his passing

Dust is my connection to my past,
        the last humble link to my parents
        in struggling my way through sorrow I missed that

My father, he embraced dust,
        heaven knows it was all around him
        he left it everywhere…

To this day, the smell of saw-dust
        still evokes sweet memories
        still brings me home

My father and mother, they found a balance, in an old-world way,
        he created the dust, she kept it under control
        kept things in harmony

So, I've learned not to hunt it, not to fear it
        to accept it as my history
        a part of who I am, of who we all are

Don't be ruled by it; don't let it weigh you down,
        But also don't run from it
        Don't treat it as an enemy

This is why things too new, too shiny, too clean,
        don't seem quite right
        like something's been lost or forgotten

So, around here, I am letting a little dust fall,
        a bit of history settle
        the beauty of age
        and legacy live on

Give me that connection to those who came before,
give me some dust…
one man's speckled monument
to his parent's love.

Jasper National Park – July 2024

CATHERINE HEIGHWAY

once the acrid **o**dour reaches nostrils
under a blood red sky that sp**u**tters and swarms with sparks
they begin to flee as survival ins**t**inct propels them to escape
overhead g**o**lden eagles
fly above nests that catch **f**ire as the flames leap
to lodgepole pine   **t**rembling aspen   balsam poplar
heat grazes tips of feathers as **t**hey circle higher in the hazy sky
elk   moose   bear   wolv**e**s find paths around the inferno
while porcupines   salamanders   **w**estern toads have nowhere to go
orbweavers scurry as webs diss**o**lve into the scorching air
on the forest floor gr**o**und squirrels burrow
delicate moss   wil**d**flowers   lichens
shrivel into **s**trands of smoke

Unquenched

V. GREGORY HOULTON

I NLAR'S LAND WAS peaceful, but his own small world was not. Leather gloves crunched and sparks flew as he gripped the tongs and pounded the red-hot iron rod straight. His land was peaceful, there was no weapons work. Not only that, but it happened sometimes that everyone's lack of a need for his forge came at the same time—the workflow of a smith was like the tide, and right now it was in a low. Work, like rebuilding the town spiriter's carriage wheel, came in steadily enough to keep eating, but just.

It kept him from restful sleep most nights, and he found himself spending more and more time absorbed in his glade.

He had been contemplating taking on work as a farrier but really didn't want to. Often the customers were as fine as the ones who needed scythes or cart axles mended, but the unpleasant ones were extra nasty.

The sharp unpleasantness of a mid-autumn morning draft prickling across his sweat-dampened back helped to keep him awake.

He quenched the steel, and the oil steamed with a satisfying hiss. Despite the fatigue in his body and being, there was still a morsel of reprieve from having done well with his hands. Feeling the morning's hard labour had earned him a try at catching a bit of sleep, he closed the forge door so no embers would pop out while he was inside.

When he hung up his apron and turned for the door, the knob pulled away from his grip. The woman's steel-coloured irises held his gaze like rivets.

"I knocked," she said, seeming relieved that he'd come to the door.

He didn't notice that she was holding up a sheathed rapier until she gave it a wave. "Can you fix a cracked blade?"

The question shook him loose from the fatigue. She was dressed far below an aristocrat, and hardly seemed the duelling type.

"Cracked?"

She gave him a mocking smile and said with a jesting tone, "I was felling a tree?"

Inlar smiled, until he drew the blade. "You must've been," he said, as his gaze trailed down the nicked and dented length, over the fracture to the bronze basket, which was so mangled it looked like wolves had teethed on it.

"I perform stage duels with my brother, as part of Duoll's travelling show. He insists it look as real as possible, so he hits hard. But not every town has a competent hot-hammer. So my wrist aches and my sword looks like a dog bone."

Inlar turned in surprise—he didn't realize there was a show travelling through. But the posters and excitement may have simply escaped his notice.

He set the rapier on his workbench. "I'll need longer to look at the steel, but I can help a little with the wrist." He went to the bucket of water he'd drawn before starting to work, and dunked a wool towel. Water ran through his fingers as he wrung it to a light dampness before laying it in front of the forge gate. "This helps the aches I get in my elbow and shoulder."

She stepped up to warm herself by the forge until the towel was comfortably hot. She bared her wrist for him to wrap the sore joint.

At the towel's touch she closed her eyes with the relief his own body understood, and it delighted him.

"When do you need it by?" he asked, already preparing himself to work instead of sleeping, convinced he'd manage.

She rolled her hand and massaged her wrist through the towel. "We're still setting up, but the show starts after nightfall."

Ache ringed Inlar's eyes as he appraised the stage sword once more. The chewed-up steel wasn't too much of an issue, but he wasn't sure about that crack. The metal told the tale of unskilled or lazy smiths who had overheated it, overworked it cold, and—in one spot—begun to actually sharpen the stage prop. "Come back as late as you can, I'll have it fixed or sorted out."

"I'll count on it," she said with a smile, and extended a hand. "Yrah."

"Inlar," he said, clasping her hand and accepting the towel back before she departed.

He held the blade once more. Even if he fixed it, the fragile blade would someday break, and hurt someone with the flying steel. But a couple hours' work was all he'd need to mend it for one show.

Inlar felt the weight of fatigue in his leaden legs, and he decided to take a short respite after all. His stone cottage was a good pace away, so that if the fire ever escaped its cage it wouldn't spread to his thatch—though he wondered how much its catching fire mattered any more.

He turned the knob and stepped into his home, which inexplicably contained a vast, open glade under a skyless expanse.

It started out much smaller. When Inlar had opened the door that first time, his ordinary dirt floor had sprouted tri-bladed grass. The more time he spent exploring this new oddity in his home— examining the grass, feeling the soil with his bare feet—the more it expanded each time he awoke in it. One day, he found that the cottage's interior walls had disappeared behind a newly grown forest. He had tried several times to find the limits of the woodlands that surrounded it. Despite travelling for what must have been hours, he found no appreciable landmarks—only an ever-deepening woods—and whenever he'd turn back the glade was still only a few steps behind him.

His furnishings were still there. The table was tucked into a bush, which grew back every time he pruned it or plucked its foliage. Inside, the front door was fitted into a large stone, but on the exterior it appeared hinged to a simple timber post-and-lintel frame. Atop a gentle hill was the heap of furs where he slept.

Inlar went past the hill to the wonder that truly captivated him, the reflecting pond on the edge of the forest.

It, too, had started much smaller, a puddle the width of his fist. Yet even then his gaze couldn't pierce its full depth.

With the ground bearing his weight, he felt that he might not have the strength to rise back up. His body vibrated like a hammer striking the anvil instead of the ingot. Inlar gazed beneath his reflection in the surface, which showed a different face than the one that stared back from polished metal in the forge.

An instant later he awoke to a pounding at the door.

Inlar forced himself upright. His head swam like he'd been drinking heavily, and his body sloshed like he was a ship in a storm.

He wiped away any grass that might've gotten stuck to his face, and pulled the door open. Yrah stood waiting, and anxious. Panic struck Inlar as he noticed the dark sky outside.

"My sword?" she asked, hopeful.

He shut the door behind him and strode toward the forge. "How much time?" he asked, though he already knew. He'd be crushed to let Yrah down, though he'd only met her that morning.

"They'll be stalling for me soon," she said, her enthusiasm deflating.

She followed on Inlar's heels into the forge. He went straight to the table, snatched her cracked rapier and twisted the pommel loose with a sharp crack. "Here, unscrew this." She took it by the handle, stuck the tip in the dirt, and leaned her disappointment against it.

He went to the incomplete carriage wheel and took one of the iron spokes. It felt like an acceptable thickness to insert into the basket.

"There's no time," she said, reluctantly unfastening the pommel with growing distress. "I need to go, Inlar."

"I just need a moment."

On the workbench he kept a pumpkin-sized clay jar filled with bondsap. That's what he called the iridescent greenish-black ooze that came from the strange brittle rocks he found in the glade.

He slid out the broken blade, and was relieved that the spoke was just small enough to fit without needing to be shaped. In a smooth motion he plunged the end into the bondsap, then slid it into the hilt. He wetted the wool towel and wrung it with a quick squeeze before wiping away the excess.

The tar-like bondsap reacted quickly to the touch of metal, emanating a faint glow and warmth as it hardened, the iridescent greens shimmering like oil in the dark ooze.

It would hold for one duel, no matter how intense.

He'd make a proper blade in the morning, and spend the rest of the day struggling to chip out the hardened pitch. He already dreaded the task, but he preferred it to leaving her empty-handed.

Inlar held the sword level with the ground, one hand on the "blade" and the other on the grip to still the spoke while the bond-sap fully set. "Hold it like this," he said, "and run back to the square. It'll be more than ready by the time you get there."

Yrah didn't look convinced, but neither did she protest. Instead, she grabbed her scabbard and headed for the door. "You're already holding it, run with me."

The glade was where he wished to be. Years had passed since he remembered wanting to be anywhere else, with anyone but his reflections. They weren't him, but they understood him best. There was wonder and comfort in being surrounded by it, and he was eager to return to his slumber.

He wanted to go, but only to help, as he never cared for the entertainment that rolled through his quaint town. He decided that he'd return as soon as he handed over the sword.

Inlar and Yrah bounded down the beaten dirt road. Even though it was just an iron spoke, his instincts made him handle it like a honed sword.

The rest of his attention noticed his heels striking the ground, and the sway of his joints in motion.

How long had it been since he'd run? Or felt the heart-pounding excitement of a hurry?

By the time they reached the crowds packed around the carnival show, his soot-lacquered lungs felt full of fire.

The long stage was a trio of platformed wagons connected end to end. A wall of black curtain hung high across the back and ran down behind the stage, sectioning off a fair-sized preparation space.

On stage, a pair of jugglers kept what must've been twenty or more wooden balls the size of apples aloft.

It was such a mesmerizing feat that even Inlar was captivated.

Barely breathing harder than at rest, Yrah took the blade by the hilt. "I'll see you after the show?"

Lament twisted like pliers in his chest. "I need to be heading back."

Her face sank with disappointment.

Inlar gave a meagre smile. "I'll watch all I can. But I'll see you tomorrow to outfit you with proper steel."

"I hope so," she said. "This may do, but it's a good deal heavier than what I'm used to." Yrah disappeared through the crowd as the jugglers finished.

They threw the balls high, letting them clatter to the stage amongst the applause.

A swarm of people in black washed across the stage, retrieving the balls and other strewn props. They hadn't quite finished when a man strode out on stage, costumed as a nobleman, complete with rapier and dagger slung from his belt. A scowl hung from a face that resembled Yrah's.

He boomed his voice like a proper villain. "Be gone! Away with you all!" As he shooed with his hands, the stage help scurried with appropriate fear, leaving nothing but the man behind.

"I am Prince Shotte, the true heir to the throne of Khessai!" he proclaimed, and went on to regale the rapt crowd with the tale of his father's betrayal and his narrow escape into exile. "I found him, too late, and my hands are forever stained by the blood I tried to staunch"—Prince Shotte examined his hands, cased in red gloves—"and I vowed my revenge."

Still dressed as shadows, the stagehands wheeled out carts and hauled out sacks to set the stage as a city street.

Inlar was fixated by the time Yrah came out as Carro, the usurper's heir.

She appeared over the top of the curtain wall, sword poised as she leaped down to strike. Shotte played oblivious so well that Inlar found himself afraid for Shotte's life. But in the last possible moment he dashed to the side, drawing his weapons as Yrah crashed down into a roll and came up with a flourish that kept her sword in motion.

Inlar realized as he watched that it was probably easier for her to obscure the dull rod for what it was, and to wield it with grace, if she didn't halt the heavy iron.

Prince Shotte indeed struck hard, playing his character to the height of anger and desperation, fighting for his life against the would-be assassin. But Inlar saw that it was having its toll on Yrah. She began to brace the back of the blade with her ungloved free hand when she parried.

Between the blows they circled, each chastising the other as an imposter, until the final clash, when the blades moved nearly too fast to track.

Shotte disarmed Carro and knocked her to her back, with a boot on her chest and his blade at her throat. "My father's throne is stolen for now, but your foul line doesn't have the strength to keep it."

When Shotte slashed, Yrah clutched her neck. Carro's death

spasm concealed her fingers tearing loose the red ribbons at her collar, which spilled down like running blood.

The crowd cheered, and when the performers bowed Inlar clapped hard enough to make his hardened palms sting. They'd earned at least as much. Looking around, he saw faces he recognized, but only as customers of his shop, or vendors from the markets he frequented, all out to enjoy the performance. They weren't the farmer, or baker, or merchant, just a delighted audience.

After the duel of Shotte and Carro, a dazzling display of fire dancers closed the show.

Inlar rolled out with the tide of people ambling back to their homes. Images of what he'd seen played through his mind. There had been other carnivals, and many were more spectacular. But on other nights his focus was too taken by the fatigue and strain to let go and enjoy the show.

As he neared his stone cottage, Inlar was contemplating what a life on the road might be like, as a smith travelling with the carnival, building props and making repairs.

Inside, the glade remained under its skyless expanse, but some of the grass had receded from the threshold, unnoticed.

Hungry Little Talbot

STACIE HANSON

HUMMING A CHILDISH tune, the boy sat in the middle of the #5 with his mother and drew a bridge on his fogged window. There hadn't been a moment where he threw himself around and screamed about unfair nonsense. He didn't snatch a phone from his mother or toss toys on the floor. When construction clogged traffic to a standstill, he didn't wail when the bus ride toward downtown stretched even longer. His happy obliviousness at first relieved the other passengers, and they wondered how the mother managed to have so well-mannered a child—but something changed soon after they met him, something that warped their relief into discomfort.

No one knew why his presence bothered them. From the moment the precocious four-year-old had stepped aboard at a crowded stop, clutching his transfer strip in one hand and his mother's hand in the other, something strange had taken over the passengers. The passengers didn't immediately notice, but he picked them off, one by one, like innocent prey. As new passengers boarded, they would find themselves taking the seat beside the boy. Sitting near him was a mistake, as the boy bombarded everyone with questions.

At first, the passengers who took a seat there found it cute, compared to their own lacklustre enthusiasm about riding the bus. But in the barrage of questions, something would settle at the back of their mind and jab repeatedly, making them itchy in their brain in a way that they couldn't quite understand. The boy would grin at them, and when they looked into his steel-grey eyes the sensation would grow. The feeling spread its twisted black vines through their brain and down to their heart until there was no ignoring the odd tightness in their chest.

With a smile, they'd leave for the back of the bus, where a quiet crowd had already taken most of the seats. They never regained those lost moments and never remembered them, only suffered an unpleasant melancholy they couldn't shake.

The boy only giggled, kicked his red rubber boots in the air, and looked out the window until his next victim arrived.

His young mother kept her eyes on the passing streets with the starved look of a tethered coyote.

The bus stopped with a groaning creak to let on an aged Black man wearing a smart tweed coat with faded cognac leather patches. As he deposited coins for his ride, he pushed thick black glasses back to cage his grey locks and looked for a place to sit. He frowned at the oddly empty front section, noticing how everyone had crowded into the rear seats, leaving only the spot beside the boy and his mother. The gentleman shrugged. A child was nothing compared to people resembling crowded sardines. He sat in a front seat with a thump as the bus hissed and chugged, the cheery robotic voice declaring the next stop, and reached into his bag for a yellow banana.

Two red boots appeared before chubby little hands pulled a small boy onto the seat beside him. "Do you like yellow?" the boy piped up. "Like bananas?"

A few seats away, his mother sighed and closed her eyes. Her elegant bearing only made the dark purple circles beneath her eyes more glaring.

Thinking she was tired of entertaining an energetic child, the man turned to the boy and nodded. "I like it fine. You?" His smile said that he liked children, and in his wallet was a faded photo of his grandson.

The boy wrinkled his upturned nose. "Nope."

"What's your favourite colour then?" the man asked.

"Hrm." The boy made a show of it, tipping his head on the side and clicking his tongue. "Red!"

"Like fire trucks?"

"Yep! Fire trucks are so tall they get stuck places. But their drivers are smart, you know. Real smart. They don't get stuck much." The boy nodded and pointed at a window. "Still like fire trucks."

The man smiled and ate his banana. But when he reached for his phone, the boy piped up with, "Didja ever get stuck before?"

The man blinked at his phone before looking up, round dark eyes now more confused than kind. How badly his chest ached— and how suddenly the pain appeared, as if someone had just come up and squeezed him hard. "Uh. Yes? I got stuck in a well trying to fix it with my Pop-Pop when I was very little, you see."

The boy swivelled in the bus seat, worn nylon and plastic squeaking as his denim overalls caught on the tiny groove between his seat and the man's. His knees poked out from the ripped holes as he brought them up to his chest. He poked the groove with a finger and a morose sigh escaped him. "Never get stuck. Bad things happen when you get stuck."

That made the man smile. "What? Like a monster will grab and eat you?"

"Yep. I live under a bridge. Things get eaten."

The boy lifted his eyes, though not his chin. Through his unkempt hair, he locked eyes with the man. A flinch curled through the man's body, but he didn't dare show it. He only leaned back in his seat and put his hand on his chest to ease the tightness in his ribs. His jovial eyes swept over that adorable face, from the chubby cheeks and olive skin to the red boots swinging with childish ease. He looked back up, only to be snared by the boy's gaze once more, and the pleasant smile on the man's lips faded.

Whatever flickered in those eyes made the man heft his bag up. "I think I see a friend in the back. Up there, see?" He cleared his throat and rose to his feet. The bus continued at speed, having found an opening in traffic. "Nice meeting you."

"You too!" With an unbothered wave and grin, the boy clambered back to his mother and snuggled into her side. She sighed, and though the man tried to see her expression, she never turned her head to him, not even to smile in apology. She simply wrapped her thin arm around the boy and stared out the wide windshield. Pushing her out of his mind, the man slipped away to the safety of those he had thought sardines before and clung to the overhead bar. A cold sweat dampened his forehead and the pressure on his chest, the itch in his brain, only eased a little with distance.

The boy rode in silence with his mother for a little while longer before he swivelled with a squeak and propped his boots on the seat. "I wanna snack."

His mother tapped her fingers on the bar. "You're having dinner. On Talbot Street. No snacks."

"But I wanna snack." He stood up in the seat and clung to the yellow bar as he stared at the top of his mother's mousy brown hair. "I want one now!"

The stomp of his red boot matched the crunching bump of the bus hitting a pothole, and the driver cursed under his breath as he swerved hard.

Her eyes leaving the street, his mother looked at the boy. Her face showed none of the indulgence of the others who had escaped. "You can wait for dinner."

The passengers in the rear of the bus shamelessly eavesdropped, and even the driver, aware of their strange behaviour, listened in. No one saw the tantrum they expected. A childish outburst would at least be normal—the itching in their brains told them so. But his next words weren't the whining of a thwarted child.

They were an ice-cold wind, the lull before a furious storm.

The boy leaned down close to his mother, nose to nose, and snapped, "I want a snack."

Even though a childish lisp softened his demand, menace coiled within the boy's words. His mother held his gaze before tilting her head a little. Everyone watched her, wondering where she was going to produce a snack from considering she held no bags.

"Really soon. I promise." His mother held out her hand, pinkie up.

The boy wrapped his own pinkie about hers and tugged up and down. "Can't break it!"

"Never do."

She looked away from the boy, though everyone still watched him to see if a tantrum loomed.

They missed the glimmer of metal and the honking, but not the crash.

The brakes screeched and the bus lurched, sending everyone smashing into one another as they clutched at their seats. With a sickening crunch of metal and the sharp shriek of tires on asphalt, the bus stopped in the busy intersection. Cutting his engine, the driver cursed and ripped his seatbelt off before flipping his doors open. The loud squeal of the doors made everyone scramble to leave, forgetting about the boy and his mother. Blocking the intersection were two cars on their sides, wheels still spinning uselessly. Other people swarmed the scene. At the bus doors, the driver moaned and cursed while the passengers filed out to gawk at the overturned cars.

In the chaos of the accident, no one noticed how the boy giggled and pressed his hand to the bus windshield with all the glee of a child at a zoo.

Once they were alone, his mother stood.

"Come on," she called. The boy giggled again and leaped down from the driver's seat as he skipped to her side. She fixed his yellow raincoat and pulled his hood over his dark hair before nodding and taking his hand. Unlike her son, she wore only her loafers and a paisley dress, fifty years too old and faded for her lanky body. Her worn face shimmered with green light as she looked out at the accident, before once again taking on the fragile paleness of someone who had once been beautiful. With firm tugs, she righted his collar and peered into his face. "Still hungry?"

He shook his head, a sly grin crossing his lips as he patted his belly. "I like snacks."

As they stepped out of the bus, she moved around the accident without seeming to care how the rain misted her dress tight to her thin body. As everyone else gaped at the damage, as the squealing warnings of emergency vehicles became ear-splitting, she and the boy walked down the sidewalk. The boy tugged once on her hand and pointed to a firetruck with hope in his eyes. She only shook her head and led him on.

As the boy and his mother walked along the wide streets, cars passed and pedestrians carried on their way, no one paying them much attention. The boy bounced into puddles, stomped and kicked, and his mother scolded him with only a bit of bite to her tired voice. Nearby, a leashed dog let loose a volley of barks that the boy only stuck his tongue out in response to. An oversized delivery truck with two men arguing about being late made him pull a bit to overhear the squabble. All the while, his hand remained in her firm grip.

Finally, they reached the last crossing, looked both ways, crossed, and then planted themselves in the southeast corner of the sidewalk. Up ahead was a bridge, neither big nor beautifully designed. Nothing more than a simple little train bridge with signs warning about the height of what vehicles could pass. When the other pedestrians on their way downtown complained that the boy and his mother were in the way, one look from her sent them scurrying away.

The boy twisted his fingers in the red buttons on his raincoat and looked up at his mother. "I'm hungry again," he said, that earlier snarl giving way to a simpering whine.

She nodded. "I know. Dinner is in a few minutes."

He grinned and nodded. "Big dinner?"

His mother looked back up the street as the rumble of an engine overtook the barking of the worried dog. "I think so. Ready?"

"Ready, ready!" he said, and he let go of her hand to plant his two feet in the ground.

"Get set."

The boy put his feet in the right position and jogged his arms at his sides.

"Go!"

His mother didn't smile as he took off at a childish sprint. No one stepped into his way as he ran toward the bridge. The overhead rumble of a passing train didn't deter him either as he ran for the dark opening, through which cars and trucks roared past at alarming speed. His mother stood there, unconcerned about sending a child alone under that bridge.

With a gleeful shout, the boy leaped to the side and straight into the bridge's sturdy wing wall. The boy's body stretched and twisted until he shimmered and disappeared. Hollow sounds of rushing air and grinding stone were all that remained.

No one saw how he simply ceased to be. The boy had vanished. A sparkle of light travelled on the walls, through the tunnel, up the rails, and down to the sign where the maximum height warned drivers. Only his mother saw him in the bridge's arches and walls. The bridge rumbled with hunger, and his mother saw how the narrow tunnel had shrunk. The warning signs beside the bridge disappeared.

That was what the driver of the delivery truck would tell the police later. There were no signs, he was sure of it. When they pointed to the biggest warning sign, he would shake his head and insist he didn't see any signs, and it wasn't his fault. The terrible tearing at the scalp of his truck wasn't his fault. The bridge had become smaller, and he didn't know how.

The woman watched the truck rumble toward the low bridge, sighed and turned away. Even the loud crunch and squeal, the devouring meeting of delicate metal against hungry steel incisors, the blast of horns, did not make her turn back. She kept moving. Her ropy brown hair slung down her back as she marched toward the other path that led down near the river.

Once on Blackfriar Street, she walked to the embankment and her feet slid over air and water as she floated, an apparition in green paisley. When her hand met the iron bowstring truss of the bridge, she closed her eyes and was glad that she was not like him, devouring trucks under the rumble of trains. Exhausted, she leaned into the truss and faded. She slithered into the trusses, melded into wrought iron and formed a beautiful arch. Soon she tumbled into the dreamless void of eldritch creatures. To rest.

Until she helped the other bridge devour steel and screams to feed his destructive craving. Her power to keep him distracted, locked away in such childish forms, could not protect the city forever. It had to happen.

His hunger was inevitable.

Out of the Blue

NANCY ABRA

T HE LOSS OF a beloved family member is devastating at any time. An unpredictable accident involving a downed plane is more life-altering. Seems like it was a lifetime ago when I received that call from Air Search and Rescue, Trenton. The memory of that evening forty years ago is still vividly etched in my mind. Had the small plane carrying Dad, Mom and their friends gone down?

Ever since my dad was a boy, the act of flying was a passion. With every noise overhead, his eyes immediately shot skyward, no matter what farm task he was doing. The desire to be a pilot never wavered as he grew older. I recall as a little girl Dad took me to an airshow at London airport. He hoisted me up on his strong, broad shoulders so I would get a bird's-eye view of the loud planes performing their skillful manoeuvres in the sky. On the tarmac, precise lines of airplanes of all sorts and sizes were on display for aviation enthusiasts to check out. It wasn't until years later that his dream to be a pilot would be fulfilled.

He worked hard in his construction business by day and once a week attended night school for the Ground School course. These classes, covering aviation regulations, meteorology and airmanship, were the first step toward learning how to fly. The rest of the evenings, when time allowed, he studied. A couple of times, he asked me to quiz him from his notes to prepare him for the test. What an honour—me helping my dad to achieve his dream. As a young teen I didn't care for school, but I witnessed my dad's perseverance. He had only a grade eight education, but he wasn't going to let that impede him. His determination to do well and succeed was an inspiration that resonated with me for the rest of my life.

With the written flying test under his belt, Dad worked on building up his flying time. He didn't waste any chance to take to the skies, logging hours to prepare for his official flight test. Finally, that day came, and we were all waiting for him when he came home from the airport.

"Did you get it, Dad? Did you…?"

"Yup," he answered with the biggest grin.

Over the next couple of decades, Dad flew various small fixed-wing aircraft. As he built up his airtime and expertise, he obtained his night endorsement and his twin rating. With these special aviation ratings, he became more accomplished. He joined the local flying club and a couple of other flying organizations. Flying wasn't just a solo act; it became a family affair. Little jaunts to fly somewhere for Sunday breakfast replaced the family's Sunday road trips. There were even a few family trips to Florida or an aviation convention—"too far to drive" was the excuse, but it was so much easier to fly, weather permitting of course.

Dad did everything by the book. He was methodical in every detail when he planned to fly somewhere, going over his maps and checking the weather. Before every flight he walked around to do a physical check of his airplane, including checking the fuel and oil in the engine. Once in the pilot's seat, he followed the plane's checklist, verifying the instruments were all in good order before leaving the tarmac's apron and heading to the runway to take off.

I knew Dad was an excellent pilot, so it was a devastating jolt when I received a phone call shortly before 7 p.m. on Friday, July 13, 1984 from Air Search and Rescue in Trenton. "We received a mayday call a couple of hours ago from a small craft registered to your father, call letters C-FAKX. A team has been dispatched to locate them. I will let you know when I have more news." As the colonel hung up, his words reverberated in my head. My heart raced. Oh my God.

❧

"I was thinking," Gren announced at supper one June evening, "Do you want to go to the Flying Farmer Convention in Winnipeg next month? It should be a good flight in our Apache. I figure it will take around ten or so hours, but I won't know for sure until I go over all the maps."

"Oh, that sounds good," Marj replied excitedly. "Maybe we could see if Vera and Bill would like to come with us. I'll call her tonight. And maybe one of the girls will take John or he could be okay to stay at home here with Dan."

Once Gren received the aviation maps of northwestern Ontario and southern Manitoba from Transport Canada, he studied them to plan his flight path. He plotted his northwest route using VOR waypoints, with the final leg ending at Thunder Bay airport. Calculating this distance, the Apache's fuel consumption, ground speed and weight and balance, Gren figured that it would be a six-hour flight to Thunder Bay, but he planned to land at Marathon for fuel and a break for everyone to stretch their legs. Even though he had been watching the weather on local news every evening for the past week for any fronts coming in, there would be no guarantee of weather until he checked the weather office at the London airport the morning they were going to leave.

The morning of Friday, July 13th was perfect, calm and clear. With the latest report from the weather office, Gren felt it was going to be a good flight to Thunder Bay, a perfect summer day for a trip in the Apache.

Gren had emphasized to Marj that with four of them in the Apache, they could only bring one suitcase between them or his weight and balance calculations would be off. Their flying companions, Bill and Vera, met them at the London Flying Club with their single piece of luggage. Marj had reassured Gren about the suitcase limit, though she also had a tote bag with essential snacks and water.

With Gren's flight plan to Thunder Bay filed with Flight Services, the Apache all fuelled, walk-around complete, they were ready to leave. Gren was at the controls; Bill, another skilled pilot, was in the right seat; and the ladies sat in the back. No one seemed to notice or mention that today was Friday the 13th.

As soon as they took off and started to head northwest, Gren set the directional gyro indicator to the compass as they flew outbound from London to the heading for the Wiarton VOR signal. This was going to be a long flight, following his planned route of the headings along the way.

Shortly after 2 p.m., they landed at the Thunder Bay airport, right on schedule, a planned stop to refuel the plane, and another break before their last leg to Winnipeg. As standard procedure, Gren called the Flight Services office to cancel his flight plan then filed his new flight plan to Winnipeg. Just before 3 p.m. they took off from Thunder Bay airport, and he set his instruments to 285 degrees heading to Winnipeg.

Fifteen minutes outbound from Thunder Bay, the plane started to run rough. He checked the instrument panel. The oil pressure gauge for the right engine was falling drastically. Gren immediately shut off that engine. With the Apache fully loaded with fuel and passengers, he knew he needed both engines to get back to the airport. Gren tried to restart the right engine a few times, but it wouldn't fire up. They were losing altitude fast.

"We're not going to make it over that ridge," Gren stated. "And with all these trees, I can't see anywhere else to land."

The plane started to shake and vibrate as Gren, with all his strength, tried to keep the plane's nose up and airborne. "We are going down. Tighten your seatbelts and brace yourself."

As they were losing altitude, the tops of the pine trees began hitting the undercarriage. Gren was still in control, but the plane was shaking uncontrollably; it wanted to stall. He wasn't going to let the airplane win. He had to keep the nose up so it wouldn't dive toward the ground. The left propeller was slicing through the treetops and branches whacked the fuselage and wings.

Both Marj and Vera had buried their heads in small pillows that were in the back of the plane. Her eyes tightly shut, Marj heard the tree branches beating and battering the plane around them—then a sickening crunch as a tree hit between the fuselage and the engine on the right wing. The plane spun around to the right. Whacking. Banging. Crunching. The sounds were deafening. Marj didn't dare look up from her pillow. The plane whirled around among the trees. Then with a jolting thud, the plane finally came to rest on the forest floor. Everything went eerily quiet.

꧁

I seemed to be in a frozen stance after the base colonel hung up, with the phone still in my hand. Before the call, I was in the middle of packing for a family holiday. That wasn't important now. I had to call my sisters and brother about the news I had just received. The colonel suggested we should all gather, so I invited them to come over. It was important to be together for the colonel's next phone call to face whatever the news.

When my husband came home from fuelling up our car, I took him aside out of earshot of our two children to tell him. He listened, a concerned look coming over his face. And then he hugged me. I melted in his arms, but his reassurance gave me strength to face the uncertain evening ahead.

Soon my siblings and our brothers-in-law arrived. They didn't say much around our children and our little brother John who was only twelve. We called a friend, and she picked up John to take him to her place for the night. We wanted to protect him from the next phone call. Whatever the news, we had to digest it first before we told John as there would be many questions that would follow. I hustled our children to bed, telling them to stay in bed and go to sleep as Mommy and Daddy were going to have an important meeting with her brother and sisters.

We all gathered around the kitchen table. Uncertainty and anxiousness mounted as time ticked on. We talked about the what-ifs, Dad's piloting skills, Mum's resilience. I didn't realize how our voices carried down the hall to the bedrooms. All this time my ten-year-old daughter had been straining to hear what we were saying. She came up the hall and called for me.

"Mummy, what's happened? I'm scared." I quickly went to her, gave her a little hug and tried to comfort her as I took her back to bed.

❧

Marj cautiously looked up from her pillow. Gren was slumped over the controls. Bill, in front of her, was moving slightly and moaning. Vera, beside her, had blacked out. She seemed to be fine, shaken but okay. She gently shook Vera, who began to come around. Outside, she could see smoke rising from the left engine. They had to get out of the plane, and fast.

The Apache's only door was on Marj's side. She struggled to get it open, and Bill helped her the best he could. Marj and Vera got out on the wing and carefully helped Bill out. They could see he was in a lot of pain. But they all persevered and got him away from the plane, gently leaning him up against a large tree. Marj went back to the airplane to get her husband. Gren was starting to come around, but she saw a small fire in the left wing engine beside where he was sitting. With a strength that was magnified by fear, she grabbed Gren's shoulder and yanked him across the seat to the wing of the plane and to safety. They sat on the ground near Bill trying to get their bearings, with broken branches and debris around them.

They were relieved when the small fire in the engine went out on its own. With instructions from Gren, Marj went back to put in a mayday call on the radio. Hopefully she did it right and her call would be heard. She needed to retrieve her tote bag. Marj took this bag on every trip, whether it was a road trip or on the plane. It was her security bag of essentials—a couple of water bottles before it was fashionable to carry water, granola bars, a couple of apples, mints, dark chocolate (as one never knows when you'll need a little treat or pick-me-up), tissues, bandages and a small bottle of sedatives, Valium to be exact. She gave everyone a tablet. Maybe that was a little illegal, but at least she felt no one would go into shock.

＊

It wasn't until 9:30 p.m., after two pots of coffee and a half bottle of whiskey had been consumed, when the phone rang. Everyone jumped, and I leaped up to answer it. The same colonel who called me earlier said, "They found them. They are in a very remote, densely wooded area."

"Are they okay?" I asked. "Alive?"

"We don't know their status," answered the colonel. "But once they send men down and clear an area with chainsaws in order to rescue them, we'll know better."

＊

Uncertainty and anxiousness mounted as the daylight dulled into evening. Surely they would be found and rescued out of the woods. The blackflies were relentless; swarms of them added to the group's traumatic dilemma.

Then, in the distance, they heard something. Helicopters?

"I'm going to find a clearing," announced Gren. "Give me a scarf, white cloth, anything. I've got to show them where we are, and Bill needs medical care."

Marj begged him not to leave them. Gren had a huge gash on his head and was still a little shaky. "We must stay together," she said. She was afraid he would stumble and black out again.

❧

Shortly after midnight the phone rang. I jumped up to answer it.

"Nancy, it's Dad. I'm at the hospital in Thunder Bay. We're all okay."

"Where's Mum…is she okay?"

"I was the first one out," he explained. "They're airlifting them out of the woods now. She should be joining me soon. Don't worry. It's late. I will get Mum to call you in the morning."

"Promise, Dad?"

"Promise," he echoed.

❧

The outcome on that Friday the 13th was devastating, but it could have been much worse. Although fate played a role, my father's calm, composed response to losing power in one of the engines contributed significantly. For decades, their story of survival, resilience and rescue out of the woods became our family's legend.

What Do You See?

STEPHANIE REISLER

L YDIA'S EYES NARROWED as she tried to read the text message on her iPhone. She adjusted her red, rectangular reading glasses and reviewed the words one by one, trying to make sense of them.

"Hey! I've got some big news for you guys. So, for the past six months I've gone by the name Iris and started using she/her pronouns. My friends all know and so do my coworkers. I just wanted to let you know before too long had passed. See you Friday."

The mobile pinged again. Lydia started. But this time it was Mel, her husband, texting from their truck outside in the crowded parking lot.

"Did you just get a voice-to-text from Ira?"

Ira was their only son and had been born blind. This weekend was his twenty-first birthday, and Lydia and Mel were out hunting for party supplies ahead of the visit.

Lydia's attention snapped back to her shopping cart. She tossed the phone into her purse, which was nestled beside a hot rotisserie chicken, and white-knuckled the cart's red handles. Overhead, a firmament of fluorescence lit aisles below flush with products, each row festooned with square white price tags. It was a material banquet for which she, quite suddenly, had zero appetite. For a moment, Lydia thought she might even be dreaming.

Outside, she saw Mel sitting expressionless behind the wheel of his truck. Lydia drew a deep breath, pulled open the passenger door and slid in along the bench seat beside her husband. She wondered who would be the first to speak. There was a loud nattering from an all-news radio station. As Mel hit the ignition and began to back out of the spot, Lydia's mind drifted through their years of parenting Ira. Had she missed signs, overlooked clues? Sure, there had been the make-believe games, costume parties, disguises, baking…Ira had even done a stint cutting material at Fabric World. Sometimes she wondered if he might be gay. But then Ira had started seeing Megan. The pair were boyfriend and girlfriend, weren't they? It was at that point she had felt they were out of the woods.

The truck lurched into their narrow driveway and roused Lydia from her thoughts. Mel cut the engine, but no one budged. The drive home had been quiet, save for the radio host who was now interviewing somebody from a trans organization about new government legislation.

"Trans and non-binary people, particularly youth, can be erased by laws that use only he and she pronouns…"

Mel flipped off the radio and turned toward Lydia, lifting the tip of his ball cap to reveal a furrowed brow.

"Why are you so upset?" he asked. Her husband seemed incredulous, his taciturn demeanour transformed.

Lydia wiped the back of her hand over gritty, damp eyes. She turned and scanned Mel's face. Was he joking? Mel wasn't exactly a barrel-of-laughs kind of guy. Something about his matter-of-fact manner triggered a weight of disbelief in her chest. She tried to speak, but then he cut in.

"I mean, if this makes Ira happier, I don't see anything wrong with it," he said. The truck door slammed as Mel marched back toward the house.

On Friday, the three of them sat together awkwardly on cream leather couches as an early afternoon sun cast a cool light from the living room windows. Ira had arrived wearing a crop top and bra that made him look surprisingly busty, high-waisted jeans and dangly earrings. Lydia wondered if his girlfriend Megan had helped with this new look. How could it be that Ira had managed to apply that black eyeliner so perfectly? As Mel droned on and on about his camping exploits and latest fishing adventures, her eyes settled on shadows of tree branches bobbing and twirling against the blank walls. Lydia didn't see how she could contribute to the conversation, but then a word suddenly surfaced in her mind.

"Brave," she said, abruptly, disturbing their chatter. "Ira, I think what you are doing is brave."

Lydia searched Ira and Mel's faces for signs of approval, but Ira's whole body had tensed, and Mel's smile had given way to an uncomprehending stare. The angry whine of a neighbour's chainsaw sliced through the silence in the room. Ira stood up, unfolded his white cane and tapped his way to the guest room. Mel followed, but then turned and thumped downstairs to the basement instead. Lydia wondered if she had said something wrong. She thought her child was plucky and bold, that's all. Had it sounded sarcastic? She suddenly craved the pleasurable, numbing effect of her go-to drink, white wine. The doctor had told Lydia to cut down on the drinking—and Mel often hid her wine—but it was how she managed her feelings when they got too big. On the way to the fridge, she heard the *Hockey Night in Canada* theme trumpeting from Mel's big-screen TV downstairs.

The following afternoon Ira suggested they all take a trip to Rainbow Falls, a provincial park close to their suburban home. The morning had been slow: Lydia had slept in late while Mel chopped winter firewood; Ira gabbed on his phone with friends. No one in the house had mentioned her remark from the previous day. The outing could be a chance to air things out. Everyone seemed keen to go.

As they climbed out of the truck into the park's dusty, unpaved parking lot, Lydia spied familiar wooden boardwalks and the long suspension bridge. The structure did not swing too much. As a little boy, Ira had loved feeling mist rise from the river below and caress his skin while hearing the churn and slap of the cascading water. Lydia often had visions during these visits. She would see people from the old Cape Mudge Indian band—before they became known as the We Wai Kai—catching salmon in reedy traps and drying them on riverbanks. She never told Mel about her spiritual sightings. But these days the river had less water; people blamed global warming. She had not had a vision for years.

On the hike, the family posed for some photos, some of Mel and Ira, and some with just Ira. Mel looked like he always did, stoic in his T-shirt and shorts no matter what the weather. Ira was wearing a red halter top, jean cutoffs and pink flip-flops. For a moment, Lydia considered posting the pictures on Facebook. Surely, that would be easier than telling her family. For a moment, she imagined millions of negative ions from the adjacent rushing waters entering her body and alleviating her near-paralyzing fatigue. But instead, a line from the theme music to *All in the Family*, the 1970s sitcom, landed like an unwanted earworm: *And we knew who we were then / Girls were girls and men were men.* She lit a cigarette and blew the smoke downwind.

As the light faded, Mel suggested they head back to the truck. Always the sensible one, she thought. Lydia liked to stay places for longer. If he was discipline, she was desire. Still, she had dinner to think of. Tall cedar trees provided a dusky canopy as they walked past giant ferns and clumps of thick, green salal with plump, purple berries. Up ahead, she could see light at the end of the path out of the woods.

Mel and Ira had stopped walking.

"Stop, no, stop!"

She heard Mel moaning—his hands shielding his eyes—as

Ira raised the white walking cane and repeatedly smashed it to the ground.

Instinctively, Lydia dashed along the path toward the pair. She stopped short of two sharp-tailed snakes on the ground. One was bleeding and looked nearly dead. The other animal was shimmying away, evoking the sound of crumpling cellophane as it wound its way through fallen tree leaves.

"I was just…." Mel's voice trailed off, breathless as he hinged at the waist, hands braced against his thighs. He stood up.

"The snakes were entwined, you know, mating. I was describing them to Ira then…everything just went haywire."

Lydia turned to look at their child but was blinded by the sun which framed Ira—now Iris—who appeared backlit, white, radiant. Lydia couldn't see it, but Iris was smiling, curiously jubilant, her strong arms outstretched wide.

Winter Astronaut

DONNA COSTA

Wrap scarf twice around, lock neck ring of hood.
Strap on backpack. Pull mask over nose.
Don fat gloves. Open latch.
Begin transfer into polar vortex.
Exit module.
Weighted Baffin boots cautiously cross threshold.
One small step.
Connect with crusty surface. Crunch.
Extreme cold. Cleats grip ice.
Path littered with moon-rocks
of snow and ice spewed by passing manned vehicle.
Aluminum pole waves flag of joint lunar mission
between Belgrade and the US — BUS.
Use Doppler effect to calculate speed and direction
of approaching rover vehicle disgorging molecular cloud.
Hop on board, pay fare.

Another day on Planet Earth.

Judges & Contributors

FINALIST JUDGE

Emma Donoghue was born in Dublin, Ireland, the youngest of eight children of Frances and Denis Donoghue (the literary critic). She attended Catholic convent schools in Dublin, apart from one eye-opening year in New York at the age of ten. In 1990 she earned a first-class honours BA in English and French from University College Dublin (unfortunately, without learning to actually speak French). Emma moved to England, and in 1997 received her PhD (on the concept of friendship between men and women in eighteenth-century English fiction) from the University of Cambridge. From the age of 23, she has earned her living as a writer, and has been lucky enough to never have an 'honest job' since she was sacked after a single summer month as a chambermaid. After years of commuting between England, Ireland, and Canada, in 1998 Emma settled in London, Ontario, where she lives with Chris Roulston and their son Finn and daughter Una. Visit **www.emmadonoghue.com** to learn more about her extensive work, including her international bestseller, *Room,* and her latest novel, *The Paris Express.*

FIRST READER JUDGES

Poetry: Andreas Gripp lives in London with his wife, Carrie. He is the author of over 30 books of poetry including *Urban Burlesque, You're Dead After School, The Lucky Ones,* and *Outré Cantata: Poems Selected and New.* His newest release is *Prodigal Planet.* His poems have been lauded for their lyrical and literary excellence and for being grounded in contemporary human experience. He was recently the Co-Director of the Black Mallard Poetry Series and the editor and publisher of the journal, *Synaeresis: arts + poetry.* You can find him at his website: **andreasgripp.wixsite.com/andreasgripp**

Fiction: Barbara Haworth-Attard is a native of Elmira, Ontario, presently residing in London with her family. June 1995 saw the publication of her first junior novel, *Dark of the Moon.* Since then, she has written sixteen novels in the historical fiction, fantasy, contemporary and mystery genres for middle-grade and young adult readers. Her latest book is, *Dear Canada, To Stand On My Own, the Polio Diary of Noreen Robertson* from Scholastic Canada. Barbara's books have been published world-wide. She has taught writing courses at Western University and Fanshawe College. Barbara has won the following awards: 2010 Arthur Ellis Crime Award for Best Juvenile; 2005 Snow Willow YA Award; 2006 B.C. YA Stellar Award; 2008 Prix Liverenette France. She was also shortlisted for the 2003 Governor General's Award; 2003 Arthur Ellis Crime Award; Mr. Christie Book Award; Geoffrey Bilson Historical Fiction Award; CNIB Tiny Torgi Award; Red Cedar Award; Ontario Silver Birch; Ontario Red Maple Award; Ontario White Pine Award; Manitoba Young Readers' Choice Award; Canadian Library Association Young Adult Canadian Book of the year Award. **www.barbhaworthattard.com**

Nonfiction: Anne Kay was born and raised in Southwestern Ontario where she lives with her family. Following stints as a nanny, waitress, and bank teller, she spent four decades working in health care finance and communication before turning her attention to her lifelong passion for writing. *The Salt Man* is Anne's debut historical fiction novel. Set in the 1800s and inspired by a true story, *The Salt Man* is a compelling tale of adventure, discovery, courage and love that illuminates the early days of Ontario's oil and salt industries. Learn more at: **thesaltman.ca**.

Nonfiction: Margaret Whitley is a speaker, writer, and Montessori consultant. She has worked in education, and today, through her writing, she promotes an educational paradigm shift to prepare children and young people with the necessary skills to face uncertainty confidently. She became a grandmother recently, which drives her determination to change educational methodology. To support her writing, Margaret graduated in 2019 with an MFA from the University of Kings. She continues to take writing courses and works in fits and starts toward an educational memoir, *A World of Difference.* Margaret's writing has appeared in several publications. **margaretwhitley.com**

Fiction: Kym Wolfe is a professional writer and editor, and former writing instructor at Western Continuing Studies. She is the author of four nonfiction books focused on London's rich history and culture: *Barhopping into History, Hopping into History: London's Old East Village, Conversations with the Artist Philip Aziz,* and *Brewhopping Across London*, and the children's picture book, *Get Outside and Play.* Her writing has been published in *The Fur-Bearing Trout... and Other True Tales of Canadian Life,* a book of short stories celebrating Canada's 150th birthday, and as feature articles in more than twenty different local and national magazines. Find Kym on Instagram at **@wolfekym,** or Facebook **@Kym Wolfe, Writer & Speaker.**

FOREWORD CONTRIBUTOR

A two-time winner of the Stephen Leacock Medal for Humour, **Terry Fallis** is the award-winning author of nine national bestselling novels all published by McClelland & Stewart. Six of them were number one best sellers. *The Best Laid Plans* was the winner of the Leacock Medal for Humour in 2008, and CBC's Canada Reads in 2011. It was adapted as a six-part television miniseries, as well as a stage musical. *The High Road* was a Leacock Medal finalist in 2011. *Up and Down* was the winner of the 2013 Ontario Library Association Evergreen Award, and a finalist for the 2013 Leacock Medal. His fourth novel, *No Relation*, was released in May 2014, debuted on the Globe and Mail bestsellers list, and won the 2015 Leacock Medal. His fifth, *Poles Apart*, hit bookstores in October 2015, was a Globe and Mail bestseller and was a finalist for the 2016 Leacock Medal. *One Brother Shy* (2017), *Albatross* (2019), *Operation Angus* (2021), and *A New Season* (2023) all became national bestsellers within days of their releases. The *Canadian Booksellers Association* named Terry Fallis the winner of the 2013 Libris Award as Author of the Year. He teaches in the Creative Writing program at the University of Toronto's School of Continuing Studies. You can find him at **terryfallis.com**.

EDITOR

Heather Godden is a developmental and line editor with twenty-five years of experience in the publishing industry. She grew up in southwestern Ontario and has called London home since 2007. She loves helping authors with the hard work of taking their manuscripts to the next level. Find out more at **GoddenEditorial.com**.

Meet the Authors

Nancy Abra, who resides near Thorndale, is an avid gardener, cultivating vegetables, herbs, and edible flowers. She is a longstanding active member of a couple of area garden groups. She also enjoys travelling and family genealogy. Besides her passion for horticulture, she has discovered an appetite for writing. She self-published a book of stories and recipes from the garden, and is a freelance writer with a garden column and articles on her community for the *St. Marys Independent* newspaper. Nancy believes everyone has a story to tell and is thrilled to be part of the London Writer's Anthology Project.

JR Boudreau is the best damn delivery driver that particular Shoppers Drug Mart location ever had. He won the 49th *New Millennium Award for Nonfiction*. His fiction has appeared in *Archetype, the Dalhousie Review, the Fiddlehead, On the Run*, and *the Puritan*.

Charlotte H Broadfoot authors short stories and poems under her own name and as Charlotte Helion, her Amazon/Kindle *Alaerton Alumni Mystery* adventure series (to date): *Reunion, Celtic Knots*, and *The Maple Blight*. Her recipe for entertaining narratives? A dash of factual history; pinch of humour; soupçon of mystic insight— blending in themes of love and friendship, animals and nature, risk and reward. She designs all cover and content art herself. A proud indie author writing/publishing (organically) mainly in winter, summer is reserved for beloved outdoor activities, art, crafts, and

'Char-B'-q-ing. For updates of Charlotte's eclectic pursuits, visit her website: **1windlass1.wixsite.com/beachcombersbookery.**

LC Browne is a writer hailing from St. Thomas, Ontario. LC's first love has always been poetry, but she is also interested in writing fiction. Joining the "7 wonders" writing group in St. Thomas and the London Writers Society has given her the inspiration to start writing again and the courage to share her words. She expresses the loss of her mother in the poem *Still.*

Krista Carson writes poetry, creative nonfiction, and fiction, often exploring nature/culture themes. She graduated from the distinguished Humber School for Writers and is pursuing a PhD at the University of Gloucestershire. Her work has recently appeared in *Motherlore, SWAMP,* and *Synkroniciti.* Krista teaches part-time at the post-secondary level, and she lives in London, Ontario with her husband, daughter, and whippet. Visit **kristacarson.com** for more.

Born in London, **Trudy Cloudt** is the eldest daughter of an immigrant family, a single mother, and a passionate educator who has spent over three decades teaching children French and Music. Her writing examines relationships, from interior family connections to external interactions and, often, the courage needed to survive them. She strives to expose the resilient, poignant, humorous moments of daily existence, employing a combination of wit and charm to entice the reader to reconsider life's not-so-ordinary moments. Trudy revives her soul in good company, nature hikes, and along the shores of Lake Huron.

Donna Costa is a former holistic health practitioner who integrates the world of natural health into her stories, including in her 2020 debut novel, *Breathing With Trees,* a YA, coming-of-age story, and her memoir-fiction hybrid novel, *If I Could Remember: Brains & Bears & Caring For My Mother,* about caregiving for her mother who had Alzheimer's (2025 release). Her nonfiction appears in *Prairie Fire, Queen's Quarterly,* and *Nurture Literary* and was shortlisted for *gritLIT* and *Event* magazines. She is currently writing a historical fiction about WWI in London, Ontario, and also working on a Nora Ephron fan fiction novella. Visit her at **www.donnacosta.ca.**

Emily De Angelis is a writer of fiction and poetry. She has short stories and poems published in various anthologies and periodicals. Her debut young adult novel, *The Stones of Burren Bay* (Latitude 46 Publishing), was released in 2024. A chapbook entitled *In the Space Between: The 'New woman' in the Writing of Florence Carlyle*, was also released in 2024 (Woodstock Art Gallery). It includes an essay and poetry by De Angelis and the paintings and writings of Canadian artist Florence Carlyle. The poem *Reunion*, included in this anthology, was written during a poetry walk along the Kagawong River on Manitoulin Island.

Michael Ross Dolan is a software developer and fiction writer from London, Ontario. In 2020-21, he was the winner of the Marie Smibert Writing Scholarship from Western University. His short story, *Parents*, was inspired by the local scenery of the Forest City, and it is the first piece he has published.

As a GenX latchkey kid, **CJ Frederick** immersed herself in storytelling of all kinds. Her fascination with language then evolved into a technical writing career. Facing pandemic lockdowns and unscheduled isolation, CJ seized the opportunity to write her first novel, *Rooted and Remembered,* which retells a true tale from her rural Middlesex County hometown about an orphan's connection to a mysterious tree. Reflecting on the alarming explosion in femicide prompted her to imagine a story about a promising life derailed by domestic violence and an all too familiar cycle of abuse. You can follow CJ at **www.facebook.com/cjtelltales** or **www.cjfrederick.com**.

Bess Hamilton's first novel, *Remembrance*, was published in 2018. She grew up in St. Marys, Ontario and attended Western University, where she earned an Honours B.A. in English Language and

Literature. After spending over a decade in Winnipeg, Manitoba, Bess now lives in an aging farmhouse in Komoka. She's inspired by local history and her lifelong love of horror and gothic fiction.

Stacie Hanson is a fantasy, Sci-Fi, and horror writer, and poet. Her writing focuses on the unknowable around us and is often inspired by the city of London. Her work is strongly steeped in eldritch creatures, twisted endings, and folklore rich narratives. You can find her online at **www.stacie-hanson.com**.

Catherine Heighway has had her poetry published with Hedgehog Press and Poetry Kit in the UK as well as in Canadian anthologies. She enjoys exploring poetic forms and in 2022 won the *Poetry Kit Ekphrastic Poetry Competition*. Catherine worked for Parks Canada and lived in the Western National Parks for many years. In July 2024, news of the forest fire in Jasper National Park became especially relevant when her nephew and his young family had to flee the townsite. These factors prompted her poem for this anthology.

Mackenzie Howson lives in London, Ontario, with her husband, soccer-loving son, and boisterous bundle of energy pup. Inspired by the people and places of Kensington Village, she wrote *Out of the Shadows on Chestnut Avenue* as a tribute to her close-knit community. Mackenzie is drawn to exploring themes of self-discovery, journey, adventure, resilience, magical realism, and choosing to do the hard thing instead of taking the easy path. She shares reflections on her personal blog (**mackenziehowson.com**) and has spent many years dabbling with writing various incomplete fictional stories. This is her first written work to be published.

V. Gregory Houlton's *Unquenched,* which is loosely inspired by the creative yearnings of a craftsperson, is the first of what he intends to be many published works. He has been a custom cabinet maker since apprenticing at twenty. Greg married his muse, and they live together in Ingersoll, Ontario, with their small zoo of creatures that fly, prowl, swim, and burrow. When not writing he can be found kayaking and tabletop roleplaying with friends and family. He can be found on Instagram **@gregory_houlton**.

Eleanor Huber has always loved words. She could read before she started school and has been writing poems for pleasure most of her long life. She loves the rhythm that well-chosen words produce. Free verse, although devoid of rhyme, still requires cadence. Eleanor taught high school English and happily introduced her students to the world's great poets from Shakespeare to Dylan Thomas. Her poem *Away* presents three scenes too often seen in our city. The poem, however, is really about the narrator who drives away, walks away and runs away. The poem is intended to evoke a response in the reader as it does in the narrator.

Barbara Johnson has always loved connecting with others through words, but it took the transformation of becoming a mother to inspire her to write poetry. She took pause from her professional career in Corporate Training to raise her young children and discovered, through many late nights of penning her thoughts, an underlying joy and talent for writing. Barbara's poetry tells vulnerable stories of motherhood, family, relationships and self. Beyond writing, she enjoys being in nature and volunteering in her community. You can read some of Barbara's work and connect with her on Instagram at **@barbarajohnsonwrites**.

Born in England, **Mari Johnson** lived in France as a teen before emigrating to Canada. She is a retired teacher and an emerging author. Mari is a longstanding member of the London Writers Society and an active member of a critique group. She is currently writing a collection of short stories.

Since 2007, **Caroline Kaiser** has been a professional book editor specializing in fiction and memoirs. She is a member of Editors Canada. Caroline is also the author of two cozy mystery novels partly set in the 1920s, *Virginia's Ghost* and *The Spirits of South Drive*. Before embarking on an editing and writing career, she worked for many years at a Toronto auction house, heading the antique silver, glass, porcelain, and toy departments. In her spare time, she enjoys drawing and baking. Her website is **www.carolinekaisereditor.com.**

Diane Kirby is a retired lawyer who lives in London, Ontario (Canada). She began writing essays to help her process the death of her husband. She also returned to university to better understand the complexities of grief. Her debut book Demystifying Grief combined her personal stories with the scholarship to explain the what, why and how of grief. Her follow-up memoir Grief and the Spirit World described her journey as she embraced her Scottish roots, Spiritualism and mediumship to further help her heal. Learn more at **www.dianekirby.com.**

Christine Langlois writes short stories and is finishing up her first novel. Set in a northern silver mining camp in the grips of a typhoid epidemic, the novel pits a young woman against the predatory mining interests of the early 20th century. Christine is also the editor and author of four bestselling nonfiction books on parenting and health and has held senior editing and writing posts at several national magazines in Canada. Her writing—both fiction and nonfiction—has won several awards. She currently lives in London, Ontario.

Adam Love writes speculative fiction that highlights our fitful relationship with culture and technology. When not dreaming of the future, he works as a virtual infrastructure engineer, writing code and crafting web interfaces that connect humans and machines.

Bruce Lord was born in London, Ontario. Published poetry in various magazines and anthologies during the latter part of the 20th century. In the early 21st century, co-authored *Humpty Dumpty Was Pushed and Other Cracked Tales*, a book of short stories for kids, and, back in the day, a Canadian bestseller. After more than a decade and a half hiatus from publishing, it is deeply gratifying to share a poem within *Out of the Woods*, an anthology comprised of so many talented and passionate writers.

In **Brenda Martin's** *Walter Mitty* version of her life, she is dashing down the Champs Elysée sporting a jaunty beret—baguette under her arm, basket brimming with fresh flowers, cheese, and wine—as she heads to her loft overlooking the Seine to compose best-selling novels on a temperamental Underwood typewriter. In the real world, Brenda creates marketing content in her home-based studio over-looking the Thames in London, enjoys the occasional glass of Côtes du Rhône, has two berets, a Trilby, and a heart full of gratitude to LWS for the opportunity to be published, at last. Visitors are always welcome at: **acreativehermit.substack.com**.

Mary Lou McRae is delighted to have her story, *Caravanning*, selected to be part of the London Writers Society's anthology, *Out of the Woods*. Her writing journey started with her retirement from a nursing career in 2010. It's never too late! Her published works include two books: *Caps & Capers* and *From Peama with Love*, both available on Amazon. She has also written several short stories and is presently working on two memoirs, *You See Me* and *Caravanning Times Three*. She remains indebted to the London Writers Society and her small critique group, who provide a nurturing environment and have suffered through early drafts of her work.

Dominique Millette is a bilingual author and translator. She has written and published three books in French (*La Delphinée*, *Car les dieux sont avec nous* and *Gouroueville*), one theatrical monologue (*L'Éveil de Sycorax*) and several short stories. In English, her por-trayal of celebrity culture in the digital age, *Better than Elvis*, came in second in *Maisonneuve* magazine's science fiction short story contest. *Oomblaug Day*, depicting the world after a zombie conquest, was published in *Parsec* magazine. *Side Gig* uses the Grimm Brothers tale of *Lucky Hans* as an illustration of toxic positivity and abdication in the face of hardship.

Martha Morrison holds a BSc in Biochemistry from Queen's University and an MFA in Creative Nonfiction from King's College at the University of Dalhousie. Her work has been published in various literary anthologies and she was shortlisted for the *International Amy MacRae Award for Memoir* in 2022. Martha is Chair for the London Writers Society anthology project and volunteers with the Humane Society as a cat profile writer. Originally from Toronto, Martha worked as a flight attendant before becoming a professional ballroom dance instructor. Martha now lives on a farm outside London with her husband, two young children and many animals. This is Martha's first published poem and she dedicates it to all the families who have been gripped by the rollercoaster of the cancer journey. Visit Martha online at **www.MarthaMorrison.ca.**

J. Edward Orchard has plied his trade as a playwright, poet, short story writer, broadcast journalist, actor, wood carver, long distance runner, instructor, dishwasher, construction labourer, security guard, customer service representative, and park-bench philosopher— sometimes even for money. He lives in the south end of the Forest City with his faithful companion, Bella, and a motley collection of tea infusers. Find him at: **jeffreyeorchard.substack.com.**

Janice Phillips is a writer and small business owner living in London, Ontario. After attempting to complete a university degree without writing essays, Janice took the advice of a professor and enrolled in an introductory English course. She discovered she enjoyed writing and earned a BA in Sociology from the University of Waterloo and a Creative Writing Certificate from Western Continuing Studies. Janice spends her time assisting in the family business (The Piping Kettle Soup Co.), coaching, travelling, working-out, and writing. *One in Fifty Thousand* is her first submission for publication.

Jayn Reed is a registered nurse with over 25 years of experience in critical care. Now a Care Coordinator at Ontario Health atHome, Jayn's journey began in the UK before she emigrated to Canada in her youth. She trained as a nurse in Liverpool, England, and eventually found her home in London, Ontario, with her husband and two boys. This short story marks her first foray into published work. Outside of her professional and writing life, Jayn enjoys participating in her book club, walking group, solving puzzles, and cherishing time with her family. She is working on her debut novel.

A former journalist and teacher, **Stephanie Reisler's** writing spans the gamut of nonfiction from daily news reporting, features and book columns to speeches, television scripts and press releases. Growing up on Gabriola Island, BC, she loved roaming forests and beaches and ferrying to the Nanaimo library to grab the latest Nancy Drew or Hardy Boys mystery. In London she enjoys drinking coffee in Wortley Village, hiking in the woods, and throwing things as a master's athlete with the London Western Track and Field Club. This is Stephanie's first-ever short story.

Jan Sims is a writer, playwright and journalist. Her short story *Girl, Lost in Thought* was published in The Humber Literary Review. Her story, *Things at the Centre of Unfulfillment* appeared in *Fleas on the Dog* online magazine. Jan's play, *Get a Life,* was the co-winner of Best Production at an international festival. Her plays, *Gracious Living* and *Weight,* were performed at The Arts Project in London. Jan's plays, *The Lost Treasure of Jesse James* and *Bed & Breakfast* were featured at the Grand Theatre's Playwrights Cabaret. Her play *A Day at the Beach* was showcased at a national play festival. Jan's career in television news includes being a reporter and anchor in cities including London and with CTV Toronto.

Al Tucker served the Canadian Transportation sector for over 50 years. He was engaged in writing articles for associated newsletters, magazines, and newspapers. Upon retiring, he was attracted to the idea of becoming a Freelance Journalist. Along with membership in the LWS, Al is a member of the St. Marys Poetry Circle. He has also written folk songs. One of his songs commemorated the 1984 visit of Pope John Paul to the Martyrs Shrine in Midland and was performed live on stage during that event. During the COVID crisis, he wrote a short story titled *Mickey Wilson & The Churchill Certificate of Courage*. It was dedicated to the families of children who feared 'the needle' and was donated to health care providers across Canada.

Heather Vanderkam is a local poet, community Social Worker, yoga instructor and mother to four amazing, unique children. Her poem *Edges of Motherhood* is based on her postpartum experience with her fourth child during the COVID-19 pandemic. Faced with the isolation and uncertainty of the pandemic, she leaned into the nurturing benefits of nature to find peace and comfort. This experience inspired her to become a Certified Forest Therapy Guide in 2022. As a psychotherapist who specializes in postpartum anxiety, Heather combines her expertise in mental health treatment with the benefits of nature-based wellness to encourage new parents, especially new mothers, to find their own inner strength and wisdom.

Laura Wythe is a teacher, artist, and writer living in London, Ontario. She's benefited so much from the advice and friendships in the LWS over the last ten years. Her short plays have been read in the Grand Theatre's Playwrights' Cabarets, and her short stories published in various magazines. In 2017, Laura published *The Bones*, a Southwestern Ontario gothic/eco-environmental novel. She has a collection of short stories coming out in 2025.

Thank You to our Sponsors

The London Writers Society is grateful for the support of local businesses, organizations, and the community, as recognized below. Their generous donations made this project possible.

In addition, we wish to thank the London Arts Council for awarding us a grant through the City of London's *Community Arts Investment Program*.

EDITOR LEVEL

Indie Publishing Group Inc.

AGENT LEVEL

King Lake Farms
Hermit Creative *in memory of Heather Schoeler*
Mituaigo Books
Ted & Reba Normile
Summum Bonum Foundation

MENTOR LEVEL

Coby & Cooper
Michael Costa
Patricia Fry & David Morrison
Barb Hall & Finn
Cynthia Lacroix
Christine Langlois
Dr. Sarah Morrison & Mark Roberts
Joan & Trevor Smith
Tuckey Home Hardware
Rudy Zimmer
In memory of David R. Frederick

FRIEND LEVEL

Phonesada Beaudrow
Better Together 177
Donna Chute
Anne Kay
Laura Konantz
Milo Mitchell
Purdham Family
Stephanie Reisler
Christopher Stocovaz
Stacie Hanson, Strut Social Design
Wendy Tippin
Alan & Karen Vaughan
In memory of Artful Art & Gorgeous George

DONORS

AARON, Michele & Ted Boniface, Susan I. Brown, Sheila Daniel,
Krista Fry, Angela Lorusso

About London Writers Society

The London Writers Society (LWS) was founded in 2007 to provide community, information and exposure for new and experienced writers in and around London, Ontario. LWS welcomes those eager to directly engage other members, as well as those who prefer to digest our resources at their own pace.

The Society is particularly proud of our inclusivity to writers at all levels. Members include those interested in writing, budding authors, writing educators, and widely-published authors. Visit the *Author Profiles* page on the LWS website to read members' biographies and explore their work.

Monthly meetings are a great place to connect with other writers and the writing-interested. The focus of each meeting ranges from guest speakers to workshops to author readings. The Society encourages critique groups who meet regularly to bring writers together with their peers for feedback on their work. In addition, LWS holds a variety of engaging events designed to inform, entertain and provide members with a platform for their work. *Out of the Woods: Voices from the Forest City,* is the Society's inaugural anthology.

Visit **www.londonwriterssociety.ca** to learn more.